HEY, I'M THE CUSTOMER

Ron Willingham

PRENTICE HALL
Paramus, New Jersey 07652

Library of Congress Cataloging-in-Publication Data

Willingham, Ron, 1932– .
 Hey, I'm the customer : front line tips for providing superior
customer service / Ron Willingham.
  p. cm.
 Includes index.
 ISBN 0-13-388158-X
 1. Customer service. 2. Customer relations. I. Title.
 HF5415.5.W584 1992   92-18595
 658.8′12—dc20   CIP

Printed in the United States of America

10

ISBN 0-13-388158-X

PRENTICE HALL
Paramus, NJ 07652

A Simon & Schuster Company

On the World Wide Web at http://www.phdirect.com

Prentice-Hall International (UK) Limited, London
Prentice-Hall of Australia Pty. Limited, Sydney
Prentice-Hall Canada Inc., Toronto
Prentice-Hall Hispanoamericana, S.A., Mexico
Prentice-Hall of India Private Limited, New Delhi
Prentice-Hall of Japan, Inc., Tokyo
Simon & Schuster Asia Pte. Ltd., Singapore
Editora Prentice-Hall do Brasil, Ltda., Rio de Janeiro

Hey,
I'm
the
Customer . . .

About the Author

Ron Willingham has headed his own training firm since the early 1960s. A pioneer in training technology, he wrote and produced the first personal development program ever recorded on audio cassettes. He was the first chairperson of the National Speakers Association's Sales Trainers Group.

He has written five books and more than 30 different training courses, including Chevrolet's Integrity Selling Program and The Principal Financial Group's Integrity Selling Program.

His firm markets *The Customer*, a seven-week customer service program, and certifies corporate managers and trainers to conduct it within their own organizations.

Another of his programs is *Integrity Selling*, a value-based, needs-focused program for salespeople and managers.

Information about his courses may be obtained by writing:

Ron Willingham
Integrity Training Systems
2425 E. Camelback Road
The Esplanade, Seventh Floor
Phoenix, AZ 85016
602-955-9090
602-955-1212 Fax

They'll be happy to explain how these programs can help your organization increase your profits, productivity and customer satisfaction levels.

From the Customer's Viewpoint

"I'm the customer. I have lots of money to spend, and I'm going to spend it with someone. I'm going to spend it on cars and clothes, services and symphonies, food and fun, books and burgers, groceries and gadgets, baubles, bangles, and beads.

"Treat me right and make me happy and I'll gladly spend my money with you. Yeah, I'll see to it that you're well paid, and that your firm prospers.

"Take me for granted, or treat me rudely and I'll take my money elsewhere. Show me you don't care and I'll quietly seek out someone who does care about me and who makes me feel important. You may never miss me, but I'll be history.

"Like I said, I have lots of money to spend. But I've got to be honest and tell you that I'm getting more and more careful about where I spend it.

"One reason is that in the last few years I've been ticked off at how I've been treated. Many people have taken me for granted and have been indifferent to me. Others have been rude to me. And some have even been downright surly.

"I'm discovering that I have lots of choices where I can buy my clothes, get my eyeglasses, buy my books, eat lunch or dinner, have my teeth cleaned, get my car serviced, buy new shoes, have my health-care needs met.

"Yeah, lots of people want me to spend my money with them.

"But, to be honest, many of them don't seem to care whether I'm happy or not. At least they don't act like they care.

"And I gotta tell you.... It'll be a cold day in Yuma before they get me back. Why should I put up with their snippiness or yawniness?

"Think I'm being unfair, and demanding too much?

"Hey, all I want is for the people where I go or call to:

Greet me and make me feel comfortable.
Value me and let me know that they think I'm important.
Ask how they can help me.
Listen to me and understand my needs.
Help me get what I want or solve my problem.
Invite me back and let me know that I'm welcome there anytime.

"This is all I want. That's it. Just notice me and make me feel important. Try to understand me and conscientiously attempt to solve my problems.

"Yeah, that's all I want!

"Hey, you take care of me and I'll take care of you. I'll spend my hard-earned money with you. I'll encourage my friends to come see you. I'll willingly come back when I need more of what you sell.

"I'll help you enjoy more money, more success, and greater career satisfaction.

"All you've got to do is satisfy me!

"This book will tell you how!"

Contents

Part II
Solving Customer's Problems 115

Part I
COMMUNICATING WITH CUSTOMERS

The Customer Satisfaction System

1. *Greet* customers.
2. *Value* customers.
3. *Ask* how to help customers.
4. *Listen* to customers.
5. *Help* customers.
6. *Invite* customers back.

Chapter 1

GREET CUSTOMERS

"PUT ME AT EASE AND MAKE ME FEEL COMFORTABLE!"

A friend and I had just finished conducting a seminar for the Georgia Bank Marketing Association at Callaway Gardens, Georgia. Having a couple of hours to kill, we drove around the incredibly beautiful gardens.

We strolled into their gift shop, which was surrounded by huge rooms of the most dazzling array of colorful flowers and plants I'd ever seen. I was taken in by the beauty of the whole experience—the brilliantly dazzling, cascading colors, contrasting with the stone architecture, laid the backdrop for a storybook setting.

Walking into the gift shop, we were approached by a beautiful, well-dressed young woman.

She walked toward us looking bored and impatient and her first words were, "We close in fifteen minutes!"

Wham! That was her greeting. Wonderful!

It couldn't have been more of a downer if she had whopped us in our faces with a wet wisteria.

All I could think of saying was, "Well...okay, we'll make sure we leave by then."

What I wanted to say was, "And...we'll try not to mess up your schedule by buying anything, either!"

She turned and walked back to her cash register—occasionally checking her watch to make sure we kept our commitment.

It happened. Scout's honor! I couldn't believe it. There, in that magnificent setting where millions of dollars had been spent on buildings, gardens, and interiors, we received that kind of treatment.

If it had been midnight at Gertrude's Greasy Spoon on the dark outskirts of the wrong side of town, I could've understood.

But this kind of an approach in that setting by such an attractive person! It didn't figure.

Now, contrast that with another experience I had. Floyd Ferner (yes, that's his real name) drives a courtesy van for Allright Parking Company in Phoenix. Now, to be honest, most rides from satellite parking lots to airports don't model exactly what you'd call excellent customer service. But that's where Floyd distinguishes himself.

He begins with a warm, friendly greeting as he jumps off the van to personally handle your luggage. The moment you're seated he hands you a piece of wrapped hard candy. A big sign in the front of the van announces, "Your driver is Floyd Ferner." And just in case passengers might miss the sign he personally announces his name over the speaker system.

After this Floyd gives the time, temperature, barometric pressure, and travel time to the airline gates. Then he announces the top three local news stories, then the three national headlines, and finally the international news.

As soon as he finishes the news rundown, he asks the passengers what city they're traveling to. As they tell him, he informs them of the temperature highs and lows they can expect in those cities. No, I'm not pulling your leg—he actually does this.

In the "Four minutes and twenty two seconds" that Floyd says it takes for him to get people from the parking lot to the airline check-in stands, he has demonstrated a case study of good customer service that most businesses could do well to notice and model.

In his own unique way he has differentiated himself from any other parking lot van driver I have ever ridden with.

The payoff? Well, I can only guess, but he seems to enjoy his job more than most people. Also, as I carefully watched him help people, I'd bet that his tips are twice what other drivers get.

From my rides with Floyd I have observed these elements of good customer service.

1. He clearly sees his job as an opportunity to serve people.
2. He enjoys it.
3. He causes people to like him and immediately feel comfortable.
4. He does something (giving away candy) that customers don't expect.
5. He impresses people with his knowledge of news and weather.
6. He makes a five minute ride an entertaining event.

Whatever you do, regardless of what it is, you too can differentiate yourself from other people. You can do like Floyd Ferner does and convert your job to a creative case study in customer service.

Being in the sales and customer-service business I naturally notice how people treat customers. I frequently go into shopping malls and visit stores just to see how I'm treated. I'm often disappointed. In fact, more often than not.

Think I'm being too harsh? How about doing your own research? As you do it, ask yourself these simple questions that several of our field people asked dozens of shoppers coming out of different businesses.

Ask yourself:

1. How well did they greet me and make me feel comfortable?
2. How important did they make me feel?
3. How effectively did they find out my wants or needs?
4. How well did they listen to what I told them?
5. How well did they help fill my wants or needs?
6. How much did they cause me to want to come back?

RESULTS OF OUR SURVEY

I asked fifteen of our field people to ask the preceding six questions informally of at least ten people as they came out of shops, stores, banks and other businesses.

Each was rated on a scale of 1 to 10, one being very poor service, 10 being excellent. Here is how the people rated the various establishments where they had just shopped:

1. Greeting and causing customers to feel comfortable   5.6
2. Making customers feel important   4.8
3. Finding out wants or needs   5.1
4. Listening to what customers tell them   6.1
5. Helping customers fill wants or needs   6.1
6. Causing customers to want to come back   6.7

As you can see, there's a lot of room for improvement. While this was an informal survey, it does seem to be reflective of the realities that shoppers experience daily.

IT ALL BEGINS WITH FIRST IMPRESSIONS

When people come into contact with you either personally or by telephone, how soon do they form impressions of you?

Turn the question around. How quickly do *you* form perceptions and feelings about people from whom you buy? And another question: What factors influence the feelings and perceptions you have?

The truth of the matter is that most of us form quick first impressions. We often *subliminally* decide whether we like people, feel good about them, or want to do business with them in the first few seconds of contact. It all happens on *unconscious, intuitive, instinctive levels.*

It happens quickly—whether in face-to-face contact or over the telephone. Someone once told me that people form *eleven* impressions of us the first *seven* seconds of contact.

That's incredible, isn't it?

Not long ago, I moved to Phoenix, Arizona, and needed to get new business telephone lines and numbers. So I called US West and was greeted by one of the friendliest voices I'd almost ever heard.

In the past, when attempting to deal with the telephone company, I was usually handled in a disinterested, controlled way that was always thinly disguised in a tone of plastic niceness. I often remember telephone people whose manner said, "Look, I'm in control. I'm trained to be nice to you, but, to be honest, you really don't have any choice about who you get your phones from. So if you don't see things my way I'll go ahead and practice my plastic niceness, but just you step outside your bounds and I'll definitely let you know who's in control. So don't waste my time any more, and let me tell you what I'll allow you to have!"

Well, this time it was totally different. Immediately, I felt comfortable. The person thanked me and put me completely at ease, almost as fast as you can say "Our dearly departed Ma Bell." She found out very quickly that she could joke with me. Within five minutes she knew what business I was in, from where I'd moved, and my telephone needs. She made me feel as if I were king of the world.

It wasn't so much what she said, it was her tone and attitude. I could tell she enjoyed her job.

She changed my whole attitude about dealing with telephone companies. Interestingly, she set the whole mood in the first few seconds. Before the first couple of minutes had passed I felt good about her, knew I would like her and was emotionally conditioned to have a pleasant experience.

Her greeting was superb and most effective.

Yours can be too. All you have to do is be aware of the importance of greeting people and then learn some simple techniques.

So, for a few moments let's think of a few simple techniques for greeting people.

GET EYE CONTACT

I could feel that US West customer-service representative looking directly into my eyes—even over the telephone!

She was totally plugged into me, despite the limitations of talking over a telephone line. We couldn't have had more rapport if we'd been face to face. She was completely focused on me and tuned in to my wavelength. I had the feeling that she caught every nuance of my voice, attitude, pacing, and emotional tone.

The moment she detected she could have fun with me she did. She also knew just how far to carry it—all within good business taste. I sensed that she was listening to much more than the words I spoke.

That's what people skilled in communications effectiveness do. They listen to people's emotions, their pace, tone, and attitudes.

Recently, I was in New York City over a weekend. In more than 100 trips there I had never attended the Marble Collegiate Church where the famed Norman Vincent Peale served as minister for so long. This time I decided I'd go.

Not knowing what to expect, I walked into the front doors of this old church building and had a most surprising and pleasant experience. Four or five people stood there greeting the people coming in.

A bit uncomfortable at first because of the lack of familiarity with this church, I was immediately put at ease by the bright, genuine smiles of those people. There was a total absence of the routine, canned greeting that you get when going into many churches.

One of the people, a man in his early forties, dressed conservatively and very professionally, with a red carnation in his lapel, said, "Thank you for visiting us today!"

His eye contact penetrated me, and his warm smile engulfed me. Instantly, I felt comfortable and knew I had made the right decision in attending the service.

After his greeting, this well-groomed, obviously happy person took me by the arm and said, "I have a *special* seat...just for *you!*" He then ushered me down and sat me in the second row.

"What a pro!" I thought to myself. Whether natural or learned, he knew exactly how to make the most of the first few seconds of contact. His freshness and enthusiasm were delivered through very strong and direct eye contact—and were made more meaningful by his obvious sincerity.

THANK THEM FOR COMING IN, CONTACTING YOU, OR SEEING YOU

Our next action guide, in addition to getting eye contact, is, "Thank them for coming in, contacting you, or seeing you."

Thank them for coming into your office, thank them for calling you over the telephone, thank them for seeing you—whatever kind of contact you have.

This is what the man with the red carnation at the Marble Collegiate Church did so well to me.

That's *not* what an attractive receptionist did the last time I went into the dental office I'd been going to for years. I walked in and stood at the counter for at least a full minute that seemed as if it were ten. The receptionist was busily recording information in a big book.

I knew that she knew I was standing there, but she didn't even look up and acknowledge me. Now, you need to realize that I'd been going to that office for thirty-five years. Frankly, I was accustomed to being fussed over when I walked in the door.

So, there I stood, not knowing whether to remain silent, fake a cough, or what.

Finally she looked up, showed no reaction to me—no smile, no warmth, no nothing—and said, "Sign in!"

Pointing to a sign-in log book on the counter, her eyes focused on the work she was doing.

She was attractive, and, I happen to know, was a nice person as well, but her inattentiveness left me feeling less than thrilled about being there. What a blown opportunity to make a memorable impression on me.

My visit was kind of a downer because for years I'd been greeted by Dona Sharp, one of the most beautiful and personable people I have ever known, who had since retired. She always greeted me, smiling provocatively and telling me that if I didn't behave myself better this visit than I did the last time, she'd have the doctor yank out all my teeth without any anesthetic.

Wow! She made my visits to the dental office pure pleasure.

Hey, all I want is to be noticed and fussed over.

TUNE THE WORLD OUT AND THEM IN

Another technique that effective customer-service people use is to tune the world out and their patients, clients, members, guests, or customers in.

They break preoccupation. They notice people. Really notice them.

In a seminar I was once doing for dental staff people and doctors, someone told me this story about preoccupation.

They said they recently acquired a new patient, and upon querying the person on why she decided to come to their office and leave the one she had been going to, they found out something rather interesting.

It seemed that when the woman had last visited her regular doctor, he had something new. When she was seated in the office, the doctor came in with a headset on. It had an earphone and a spiral cord that trailed down through his belt loop and dangled there.

He came into the operatory, washed his hands, routinely spoke to her, and began his work. Upon doing this, he plugged the spiral cord into a telephone jack, popped an automatic dialing card into his telephone, and began a conversation with his stockbroker while examining the patient.

Now wasn't that a warm experience for the patient?

Well, needless to say, she was underwhelmed.

The doctor had probably been to a recent time-management seminar and thought he was making the best of his time. Or, maybe he was just bored at having to look into people's ugly mouths. Whichever, it definitely cost him at least one patient who took her mouth and checkbook to some other dental office.

Now, you say, "Oh come on, I would never be that blatant." And, of course, you probably wouldn't. But how often do we *mentally* talk to our stockbrokers when we should be focusing on our customers?

It's called preoccupation. Preoccupation is thinking about something else rather than about the people in our here and now. It's very easy to do unconsciously and can be very damaging to our customer relations.

GOOD CUSTOMER SERVICE SKILLS BUILD SELF-CONFIDENCE

As I view the thousands of people who go through my *Customer* program, I see clearly that good customer-service skills and self-confidence are interrelated. They both go together.

Taken a step further, let me assert that as people increase their customer-service skills, their self-confidence automatically goes up. I see this proven true all the time. I get many letters from people who back up my claim. Like Cathy Hudson of Thompson Dental Supply in Raleigh, NC. Cathy writes:

> Your course helped me to learn how valuable the customer is and how important my attitude toward the customer is. People now ask for me when they need help or want a problem solved. It has made me feel good about myself *and* has given me more confidence...

Confidence is feeling good about ourselves, and it's something we all want to develop in greater dimensions.

Or, here's an excerpt that Eli Estreicher of the Jewish Community Center of Birmingham wrote in a letter:

> ...I have noticed a gradual, but steady, professional and personal growth and development trend, shared by all the participants in your *Customer* program.

> I have seen the participants perform their various tasks at the Center in a more competent, confident, patient, communicative and caring fashion.

> Additionally, customer service trainees are exhibiting enhanced techniques in relating to customers, providing quality service, setting priorities and solving problems effectively.

IN SUMMARY

Let me summarize what we've been talking about by emphasizing that a lot of selling or communication takes place during the first few seconds of contact you have with your customers. Feelings and perceptions are formed that are often lasting ones.

Your eye contact, your attitude, your ability to break preoccupation, tuning the world out and the person in have immediate impact on people.

It can't be explained with logic; it all happens emotionally.

Your nonverbal gestures, body language, and facial expressions make quick subliminal impressions on people.

Customers are going to say to themselves unconsciously, "I like this person," "I feel good about this person," "I want to do business here."

Or, subconsciously, they may say to themselves, "I don't feel comfortable here," "This person isn't really interested in me," "This isn't a place where I want to do business."

Yes, it all begins with the way you *greet* people. So much happens the first few seconds.

Your sincerity, genuine interest in people, excitement with who you are and what you do—these are the causes that produce the effects of putting people at ease and making them feel welcome.

Go out and do your own research. Check out places where you spend money. See how little these common courtesies are done. Then notice how great you feel when someone greets you properly. Notice how you feel when people say with their actions, "Hey, you're the customer...you pay my salary!"

So if you want to stand out above the crowd, practice the action guides of this chapter. Practice, practice, practice them until you do them unconsciously.

You'll then make the most positive impact on people.

You'll consistently put people at ease and make them feel comfortable!

HOW TO GET GOOD AT GREETING PEOPLE

1. Get eye contact.
2. Thank them for coming in, contacting you or seeing you.
3. Tune the world out and them in.

SOMETHING TO THINK ABOUT

People average making *eleven* decisions about you in the first *seven* seconds of contact !

CHALLENGING YOUR WAY OF DOING THINGS

Want to have a very productive week? Sit down by yourself for one hour and do nothing but think—not that this is exactly easy to do.

Say over and over to yourself, "There's a better way for me to do my job than the way I'm now doing it, and I'm going to discover it!"

Then think about and get angry at statements you've heard yourself and others around you make, such as:

"We've never done it that way before!"

"We've tried that and it doesn't work!"

"Our customers are only interested in price!"

"Most people who come in only waste my time!"

Yeah, sit down and get steamed. Get angry at the routine that has developed around you. Challenge your old ways of doing things. Get worked up into a white-hot lather. Throw out old nonproductive, non-customer-focused ways of doing business!

Make some changes. Do something creative that cuts out useless activities and helps you focus on customers' needs.

DAILY SUCCESS DIARY
GREET CUSTOMERS

Performance is always improved by evaluation!
After you've read this book completely through, please come back and spend one week rereading and practicing the ideas in each chapter. This concentrated focus will help you develop strong successful habits.

Each day evaluate your performance. On a scale of 1 to 10 rate how you practiced the action guides.

	S	M	T	W	TH	F	S
Greet Customers							
1. Get eye contact							
2. Thank them for coming in or contacting you							
3. Tune the world out and them in							
Total each day							
Daily average per week							

Chapter 2

VALUE CUSTOMERS

"LET ME KNOW THAT YOU THINK I'M IMPORTANT!"

The attractive, well-trained American Airlines ticket agent scanned my ticket, pecked several letters into her computer, pulled my old boarding pass off, and stapled a new one to my ticket—upgrading me to first class.

I thanked her and told her how much I appreciated her kindness. She smiled warmly and said, "Well, Mr. Willingham, without loyal customers such as you, I wouldn't have a job!"

Wow! The encounter lasted only a few seconds, but I came away feeling as if that whole airline was dependent on me for its economic security. I was tempted to quadruple my life insurance because of my newly elevated level of importance.

Contrast that experience with the one I endured on United Airlines. I had flown from Fresno, California, to Chicago at O'Hare. No food was served. We arrived at Chicago about 7:00 P.M. I had a connecting flight in forty minutes to Atlanta. I had been conducting a seminar and had eaten only a light lunch.

Rushing to the ticket counter to check in for the Atlanta flight, I asked the agent if the flight to Atlanta was a dinner flight. After checking she told me that no food would be served.

Without irritation I said, "But I just came in on your flight that didn't serve food, and if this one doesn't either, how am I supposed to eat?"

I thought I said this in a pretty nice tone of voice; at least I tried to do so. She looked at me and snarled, "Look, I don't make the rules! There are food courts down the terminal! I have this long line of people to check in!"

Then she flicked her left hand and motioned loud and clear: Move along, unimportant person; I have more important things to do than to mess with the likes of you!

Her rudeness even surpassed the old Braniff ticket agents at O'Hare, which would be generally regarded as next to impossible if you ever experienced the Chicago Braniff people—who were exceeded in rudeness only by the Budget Car Rental people there.

Guess which airline I'll favor flying in the future?

One ticket agent saw customers as people who made her job possible. The other saw them as annoyances.

One communicated, "Hey, you're the customer, you pay my salary!"

The other one's actions broadcast: This job would be OK if I didn't have to deal with so many *dumb* people.

One clearly *valued* me. The other didn't.

The key word is *value*.

VALUES GO DEEPER THAN MERE TECHNIQUES

Using the different words *values* and *valuing*, let me say that *valuing* people goes much deeper than just focusing on techniques and strategies—it's actually a *value we have*. It operates from deeper levels within us—our attitudes and motives—*our* values.

For a few minutes let's think about three important areas that impact how well you do with customers. They are:

1. Attitudes
2. Motives

3. Values

My *attitude* is the way I think. It's reflected in the way I carry on my work. It's shown in the manner in which I relate to other people. It's also demonstrated in times of stress.

My *motives* are the reasons why I do things. I may work hard, be diligent and congenial because I feel good about myself when I do. Or I may perform my work in these positive ways because I enjoy the recognition and positive feedback I receive when I do. I may even work hard and increase my job efficiency because I want to earn more money or get a promotion. All these are motives—reasons why I do things.

My *values* are inner guidelines that direct my behavior. Values are rules by which I live my life. Values guide behavior. My behavior is almost always consistent with my values; I won't do things that conflict with them.

What do these have to do with good customer service?

Everything!

Good customer service isn't just painting a smile on your face and performing certain plastic actions because you're expected to do so. People can quickly see through these thinly veiled attempts at niceness.

VALUES DRIVE OUR ATTITUDES, MOTIVES, BEHAVIOR

It's important to understand this truth: Our values drive our attitudes, motives, and behavior.

So, what does all this mean? And why repeat it twice already?

OK, here's the reason I emphasize the point. Read this several times. Then underline it and put asterisks on both sides of it.

When our values are right, our attitudes, motives, behavior will be right!

Think about that for a few moments.

It's true! When our values are right, everything else will be right.

Sound too simple? No, read on.

Here are three *values* that, when internalized, will almost always guarantee success with customers.

1. Think, "You're the customer—you pay my salary!"
2. Think, "There's something about you I like!"
3. Think, "You make my job possible!"

"YOU'RE THE CUSTOMER—YOU PAY MY SALARY!"

When this is a value of mine, I'll just naturally make my customers feel important. My actions will be automatic.

But check around and you'll see that many businesses or professional offices don't always demonstrate this value to you.

At least they didn't know how to do it at a doctor's office I went to not long ago.

My problem was that for two years I had a plantar's wart on the bottom of my foot, where most of my weight is put. (Thrilling subject, isn't it)? For two years it was like standing on a pebble whenever I did seminars—which was most of the time.

Finally I scheduled an appointment with a podiatrist for 2:00 one afternoon on a free day when I was in town.

I got to the doctor's office, signed in, and was told to be seated and that I would be called when the doctor was ready.

Thirty minutes went by. I quickly read all the magazines. I asked the receptionist if she had any idea when I would get in, that I was very busy and couldn't afford to waste time. She replied, "Oh, you never can tell...you know how doctors' offices are."

Frankly, I wasn't too thrilled with her words or her lackadaisical attitude.

Another thirty minutes went by. I asked the same question and received the same reply, "Oh, you never can tell, you know how doctors' offices are."

I wasn't any more thrilled this time. My mind flitted from one crisis to another that I needed to be solving at the office. Then another forty-five minutes went by. I'd asked twice more and got that same unconcerned, yawning reply. So I returned to my chair, ticked off that this person was messing up my afternoon.

Then something wonderful happened...I thought. I was moved into a treatment room. "Oh goody," I brightened up, "Now the doctor will come in and see me." I was told to take off my shoes and socks so as to save the doctor's time when he came in. Ecstasy and warmth quickly filled my heart—just knowing that I would save the doctor a few seconds of his precious time.

It was another thirty minutes before he showed up, and I had to sit there and look at my gross, gnarled, ugly feet—ugly *cold* feet.

Finally he came in. Check it out—two hours and fifteen minutes after my appointment.

"And how are you?" he gushed as he breezed in.

"Not too well, frankly," was my response.

"Oh," he asked, clearly not interested in my response, "Why not?"

"Well, I had an appointment at 2:00, and it's past 4:00 now."

Looking at me as if his words were about to totally salve the situation, he shrugged, "Oh well, you know how doctors' offices are."

I was irritated at his complete disregard for my time. My only response was, "No, now that you mention it, I *don't* know how doctors' offices are! How are they?"

He pulled his nose in the air, flared his nostrils and peered over me as he magnanimously overlooked my tacky, selfish response.

Did he *value* me? Did his yawning receptionist *value* me? Did either realize that I paid their salaries?

Within two minutes he had looked at my foot and told me what he would do and how much it would cost. At that moment I told him what he could do and what it would cost him—my business and good will.

He looked bewildered as if to say, "I don't appreciate your attitude. I'm the doctor, and it's obvious that you aren't educated enough to know that everyone should bow and worship Wonderful Me."

Well, I hoped it wouldn't completely ruin his life, but I wasn't about to waste my worship on him!

"THERE'S SOMETHING ABOUT YOU I LIKE!"

When dealing with customers we usually have two choices.

1. We can choose to focus on what we like about them, or

2. We can choose to focus on what we don't like about them.

It often comes down to a simple choice we make.

Just the other day I was eating in a nice, upscale seafood restaurant. A small, thin man, who looked to be in his seventies was seated at the table next to mine. The waiter, a young woman in her twenties, came over and exclaimed, "Oh, Mr. Goldman, it's so good to see you again."

She then sat down by him, took his hand, and said, "How have you been feeling since your surgery?"

It took only a moment for her sincerity to impress me.

The customer brightened up and for a couple of minutes gladly told her how he'd been feeling. She patiently and empathetically listened. Watching the scene, it struck me that she really cared about how he'd been feeling. It wasn't just an act she was putting on.

Momentarily, she excused herself, went about her other duties and then returned to take his order.

My mind couldn't help filling in the blanks. Here was a lonely person whose needs weren't just to have a pleasant dining experience, but to be noticed and fussed over. To have someone listen and show genuine concern.

As I sat watching him beam and enjoy the attention he was getting, I couldn't help wondering if the restaurant manager really knew why Mr. Goldman chose to return. He probably thought it was their menu. I also wondered if he fully realized what an asset he had in the young lady.

I watched her greet and serve other people, and while most didn't get the same treatment as Mr. Goldman got, all felt her sincerity and friendliness.

She enjoyed her job. She sincerely focused on what she liked about people.

It was a choice she had made.

"YOU MAKE MY JOB POSSIBLE!"

Now bear with me and let's think again of the three words I mentioned earlier in this chapter: *Attitudes, Motives, Values.*

My *attitude*, or *how* I think, is influenced by my *motives*, or *why* I do what I do. Both are then driven by my *values*, or *what's* important to me and what guides my choices and behavior.

When my values are right, my motives and attitudes will be right. It's cause and effect.

"OK," you say, "you've repeated yourself. So assuming this is true, then what *values* do I need to have in order to cause my customers, patients, or clients to have a satisfying experience?"

Let's think about this for a few moments. Let's begin by asking a most basic question. The question may be basic, but few people know the answer.

"WHAT BUSINESS AM I REALLY IN?"

What do I mean? Am I talking in simplistic riddles?

No, my experience tells me that most people who work with people don't really know what business they're in. Most think they're in business to *deliver products or services*. They don't know that they're in the business *to give end-result benefits to people*. Think about this a moment and you'll see that there's a big difference.

A receptionist at a medical doctor's office may think she's there to schedule appointments. He or she is really there to greet people, make the most of the first few seconds of contact, to put them at ease and let them know that they've chosen the best place to come.

A clothing salesperson isn't in the business to sell clothing. Actually he or she is there to identify people's needs, find out what budget they have, what occasion they want the clothing for, and help them present a desirable image.

A jewelry salesperson isn't there to sell people rings and diamonds. He or she is there to identify dominant buying motives and then to help people realize their dreams or to make other people happy with their purchases.

A hospital nurse isn't there to check on patients and record information for the doctors. He or she is there to help people enjoy as much comfort as possible, relieve anxiety, and reassure family members.

Here's my point:

You're *not* in business to sell or deliver products or services, you *are* in business to help people enjoy end-result benefits of those products or services—to enjoy as much satisfaction as possible.

If this is a belief of yours, a *value*, then your motives and attitudes will be congruent. You'll be centered and focused. You'll say and do the appropriate things to satisfy your customers.

IN SUMMARY

The second step of our Customer-Satisfaction System is: *Value* the customer.

Techniques and strategies without appropriate motives and values will always fall one step short of total success. Painting-a-smile-on-your-face type techniques seldom work.

The real secret of success with customers is to have the proper *values*. To have inner guidelines that say, "My job is to give total satisfaction to customers."

It's to say, "I see my job as being more than selling or delivering products or services. I see it as helping people enjoy end-result benefits."

With this value, we see our jobs differently. We view customers, guests, or patients differently. And the paradox is that we also view ourselves differently. We like ourselves more and enjoy what we do more.

Yes, the payoff of doing others-focused activities is that we enjoy exciting personal rewards. One of the rewards is increased self-respect, and that's one of the nicest things that can happen to us.

Yeah, the truth is that as we grow in self-respect, we always prepare ourselves for greater things ahead!

HOW TO GET GOOD AT VALUING PEOPLE

1. Think, "You're the Customer—You Pay My Salary!"
2. Think, "There's Something About You I Like!"
3. Think, "You Make My Job Possible!"

SOMETHING TO THINK ABOUT

When you value people your sincerity causes them to feel good about you and trust you.

ASSESSING YOUR OWN VALUES AND MOTIVES

Want to do something that may be uncomfortable? Maybe even threatening and disturbing?

Get a hand-held mirror or go stand in front of a large one. Read these questions to yourself and then look into the mirror. Get an eye lock and then ask them of yourself again.

"What's the real reason why I do what I do?"

"What are some *values* that guide my behavior?"

"Do I see my job as just a job, or do I see it as a way to create value for people?"

"How can I cause each customer to remember me and feel good about his or her contact with me?"

As you ask these questions of yourself, looking deeply into your eyes, you'll not only assess your own customer-service values, but you'll also challenge yourself to constantly improve your performance.

DAILY SUCCESS DIARY
VALUE CUSTOMERS

Good customer service begins with proper attitudes and values. Our actions are usually the result of our motives and intentions. When we value customers we'll usually show it.

As you practice the action guides and scan this chapter each day of this week, take time to evaluate your performance.

	S	M	T	W	TH	F	S
Value Customers							
1. Think "You're the customer—you pay my salary!"							
2. Think, "There's something about you I like!"							
3. Think, "You make my job possible!"							
Total each day							
Daily average per week							

Chapter 3

ASK
HOW TO HELP
CUSTOMERS

"FIND OUT
WHAT I WANT!"

I went into a Ralph Lauren Shop to buy one suit; I left with three, along with shirts, ties, and other accessories.

I was approached by a salesperson while I was flipping through the suits. "Have you been into our store before?" he asked.

He didn't ask the typical question, "May I help you?" So I didn't give him the standard response, "No, I'm just looking," as most people do when sales or service people ask them that worn out question that reveals their lack of training.

"Yes," I replied.

"Are you looking for anything in particular...or would you just like to browse?"

"Well, I'm kinda looking for a new suit."

At this point most salespeople say, "42 long, heh?" and point to the suits that size, hoping I'll pick out one I like. If I seem to like one they'll usually try to sell it to me, whether it's right for me or not. But not this young man.

"What occasion do you want a suit for?" he asked.

"I conduct training seminars," I responded.

"Oh, what kind of seminars do you conduct?"

"Sales and customer service."

"Well, that's interesting. What kind of people do you conduct these seminars for?"

"Oh, all kinds of companies. Anyone who wants to sell more or improve their level of customer service."

"Where do you do most of these?"

"All over—East Coast, West Coast—and everywhere in between."

"So it's important that you present a very professional image?"

"Yeah, it is..."

"Are you wanting to replace some old styles or colors?"

"Oh, not really. I need something in dark colors—navy, charcoal, dark gray—something like that."

Within a few minutes he knew what I wanted, how I was going to use it, and the image I wanted to present at my seminars. I pulled out a couple of suits and was advised that the cut of them wasn't right for my build. He then showed me a navy suit that was much more expensive than the ones I had looked at. He explained why it was a much better buy, which all seemed very logical to me.

I had mentally bought the navy suit when he showed me a gray pinstripe, saying that it would complement the other one nicely. Then a beautiful blazer. Then several pairs of slacks. Then shirts, ties, pocket squares—all coordinated so everything went together.

He was fussy and nit-picky about the alterations—bragging to me about the skills of Miguel the tailor, and bragging to Miguel about my tastes and professionalism.

It was a most pleasant experience—all because he took the time to really understand my needs. His whole objective seemed to be to help me select and put together clothing and accessories that would package me professionally. I felt as though I could trust him.

Sounds simple, doesn't it—how he took time to first understand my needs?

And, of course, it is simple...although few people take time to do it.

It's so simple that I always wonder why so many people don't do this customer-focused approach. In fact, most skip it completely.

Many people, whether they're in retailing, telemarketing, medical offices, or other places where people spend money, don't seem to know how to identify the real needs customers have.

Maybe they've never been trained how to do it. Read this chapter carefully and apply the suggestions and you'll know more than most other people know.

IDENTIFY NEEDS

How do you go about identifying people's needs? Let's think about it.

First, please understand that our needs aren't for the product or service! Rather our needs are for what the product or service will *do* for us. The end-result benefits it'll give us. How it will help us be happier, healthier, wealthier, wiser, or more beautiful.

Remember, it's important to understand that people don't buy products or services. They buy products or services in order to fill needs they have, satisfy wants or gratify desires they have.

Patients don't have their teeth cleaned just so they can have clean teeth. They do it so they can be more attractive, enjoy better health, or prevent future problems.

Customers don't buy automobiles just to have a vehicle to drive. They purchase to please their families, keep up with the Joneses, get good gas mileage, or save money.

People don't spend money on cosmetics because they have to have cosmetics. They do so because they want to be more attractive, appealing, or enjoy more recognition.

People don't just go to restaurants just for the quantity of food. They go because of the atmosphere, unique preparation, or dining experience.

Get the picture? People don't buy what you sell because of what it is or how it's made or how you do it (if it's a service). They buy what you're selling because they want to enjoy an *end-result* benefit for *themselves*.

So, a most important part of your contact with customers will be to find out what their needs are—find out the *payoff* they want from what you sell. Here are three action guides for accomplishing this step—for finding out how you can help people.

1. Ask, "How may I help you?"
2. Find out why they came in or contacted you.
3. Ask open-ended questions to further understand their needs.

Ask, "HOW MAY I HELP YOU?"

After you have greeted your customers, patients, members, or guests, and after you have mentally reminded yourself of their value to you and your firm, then find out how you can help them. Find out how you can heal their hurt, fill a need, solve a problem, or satisfy a want they have.

Now, you probably won't use the above words, "How may I help you?" or you may; it all depends upon the nature of your business or profession.

Your main objective is to focus on understanding what they want. Clichés such as, "May I help you?" if you're in retailing aren't as complete as, "How may I help you?" One calls for a quick turn-off response; the other calls for an explanation.

Words aren't important; they vary from one profession or business to another. What's important is that you get information that helps you understand people's needs.

When you want to find out how to help someone, your words will be right.

FIND OUT WHY THEY CAME IN OR CONTACTED YOU

One of my friends was in banking for several years. He loves to tell the story of this elderly man who was very modestly dressed coming into one of their branches asking if the brochures and bank reports on the check stands were free. Being informed by a teller that they were indeed free, he thanked her quietly, took some brochures, and left.

It wasn't long before he came in again. In a very unassuming way he asked if he could have some of the free matches and if there were any other free advertising pieces.

He was given some and left. His visits didn't exactly cause the bank to shoot off sky rockets, spend a day celebrating, or declare special dividends to its stockholders.

After that he was in a couple of times, very quietly asking questions of different people. The bank employees began talking about him because his appearance certainly wasn't one of wealth and prosperity. They just assumed that he was a poor old man who, having lots of time on his hands, spent it asking for free samples of advertising and brochures.

Then one day he came in asking about interest rates and asking if he could see one particular person who had always been nice and courteous to him. When he was seated at this person's desk he had her transfer several hundred thousand dollars from a bank in Florida to this one.

Everyone was shocked.

Reflect on the story and you'll clearly see that he had a reason for coming in. A reason that probably few, if any, of the employees took time to discover. No one took time to find out information about him. But they could have easily identified his needs if they'd asked the right questions.

Several years ago I received a letter from a bank teller who was involved in one of the training courses that my friend Bernard Petty was conducting. She shared a most impactful lesson she had learned.

She told of an elderly woman who for several years had come into her bank each month to deposit her Social Security check. The woman was always dressed up and took several minutes just to visit with the teller. While the bank teller always enjoyed the visits, they weren't exactly the most important events in her month.

One particular month rolled around, and when the woman came in, the teller told her about the new drive-up windows. She explained how it might be more convenient to use them rather than having to come into the main bank building.

When she told the woman this the woman looked very distraught and replied, "Oh no, I would never want to do that!"

She then went on to tell the bank teller a story that almost blew the teller away. She told the teller that she lived alone on the edge of town. She explained that she got out of her home only once a month to come and deposit her check at the bank.

The bank teller was overcome when the woman told her that she planned all month long what she would wear on her next trip to the bank. She told her how eagerly she looked forward to the following month's visit and that it was her *only* social contact.

Then she stunned the teller by saying, "And...you're my best friend in the whole world!"

Wow! What an impact this had. The teller learned a whole new lesson about what business she was in. And, where heretofore she had assumed that people came into the bank only to do banking, now her entire perspective changed.

Why *do* people come in to see you? Why *do* customers call you? What are their real reasons? What customers do you have who might just view you as their best friend?

How good are you at finding out answers to these previous questions? How much effort do you make?

When you know *why* specific people come in to see you, or contact you, you can better understand their individual needs.

Ask OPEN-ENDED QUESTIONS TO FURTHER UNDERSTAND THEIR NEEDS

It's logical that we can best help customers when we understand their needs. Their needs being *what* they want, *why* they want it, or *how* they plan to use it.

Remember—people don't buy products or services just to have the products or services. They buy them in order to satisfy needs, fulfill wants, solve problems, or gratify desires.

So part of your role in satisfying customers is first to understand their needs. You do this by asking open-ended questions. They get you lots of information. Open-ended questions are ones that call for explanations. Closed-ended questions are ones that call for "yes" or "no" responses. They don't get much information for you.

If you're selling automobiles, you'll want to understand how people use their cars or trucks. You'll want to know what they've been driving and how they liked it, or who else will be driving it. You'll want to find out the special features they want. If you're a service writer you'll want to know what problems people have experienced, when they first began, and what the symptoms have been.

If you're a dentist or dental assistant, you'll want to identify whether patients want to improve their appearance, relieve pain, fix a functional problem, or prevent future problems. You'll probably want to understand their degree of dental awareness.

If you're a rental car reservations person you'll want to know what size car a person wants, how long they want it for, and how many miles they'll be traveling.

Get the picture? Learn to ask open-ended questions to understand people's needs. Open-ended questions are ones that contain the words, *who, what, where, why, when, how.*

Not only will these questions help you get information to understand a person's needs, you'll also strengthen your rapport by showing your concern and actively listening to him or her.

PEOPLE'S NEEDS AREN'T ALWAYS LOGICAL

Sometimes people's real needs have little to do with logic. Often they're emotional. It may be that people who contact you or come in to your business are unsure of what they want. Or they may be afraid of the buying or servicing process.

Many people are confused by product claims. When it comes to getting their car or appliances serviced, they feel very inadequate in communicating with service advisors or repair people.

I wrote and designed Chevrolet's Integrity Selling® Program, and one thousand dealers were trained to conduct the program for their sales and customer service people. In listening to their customers we faced a gigantic problem of which they seemed totally unaware. The simple fact was that people are terrified of the car shopping/buying/service experience.

We helped salespeople understand this and to ask sensitive questions that got customers talking about those fears.

After installing our program in one of the largest volume dealerships, Friendly Chevrolet in Dallas, I walked into their showroom a month or so later. One young salesperson yelled at me and then came running over to me.

"It works, it works!" he shouted excitedly.

"What works?" I asked

"The question."

"Which question?"

"The fear question," he responded.

Then he told me this story.

A young, single career woman came into his dealership. He approached her. She was closed, suspicious, and defensive. It was obvious to him that she was resisting him. He asked her to come and sit down in his office so he could ask a few questions that would help him better understand her needs. She did, reluctantly.

He asked her questions like, "What kind of car have you been driving?" "How do you use your car?" "What are some features you want in a new car?" "What have you looked at so far?"

He still sensed that she neither felt comfortable nor trusted him.

Then he asked her *the* question. He asked, "What unpleasant experiences have you had in shopping for cars in the past?"

She paused a moment or two and then burst into tears. He patiently listened as she told him of being hustled, hassled, and propositioned in other dealerships. She then told him of her fear of the experience.

She talked for an hour. He kept her supplied with Kleenex tissues and just listened.

Then she sat up, thanked him for listening and caring, and in essence said, "You're the person I want to buy my car from because I know I can trust you, and you aren't like all those others."

He was perceptive enough to ask the right questions that helped him discover her real needs—the need to deal with someone she could trust. Price wasn't at all the dominant factor, even though she'd previously told him it was.

Remember, people don't always think or decide purely for logical reasons. They are frequently influenced emotionally—by fears, need for recognition, selfish motivations, momentary moods. People are often motivated illogically.

Asking open-ended questions will not only help you understand people, but it can help you demonstrate your concern and care for their needs. Asking these questions and listening to people's responses can help you enjoy trust and rapport with them.

When you develop trust with people you'll find they'll accept your ideas better and will want to return to see you.

IN SUMMARY

The action guides in this chapter will help you demon-strate your professionalism and concern for people. When you really want to understand people's needs, and carefully ask questions to make sure you do, you'll quickly impress them.

Then, when you do understand *what* people want, *why* they came to see you or contacted you, you'll just naturally be in a better position to help them.

Remember these six important words to use in your need-development questions. They are: *who, what, where, why, when, how.* Ask them and you'll get a lot of information. And with that information you'll better understand people's needs.

Your patient listening, along with your care and concern, will impress people and cause them to want to buy from you or return to see you.

HOW TO GET GOOD AT ASKING HOW TO HELP PEOPLE

1. Ask, "How may I help you?"
2. Find out why they came in or contacted you.
3. Ask open-ended questions to further understand their needs.

SOMETHING TO THINK ABOUT

A genuine desire to understand people's needs or wants impacts customers and places you ahead of most other people in your field.

RECOGNIZING NEEDS PEOPLE HAVE

Want to maximize your contact with each customer? Want them to be impressed with your care and concern for them?

First, remember that people have different needs, and when their needs are met they'll want you to continue helping them in the future.

Here are some of your customers' needs:

1. To be valued by you.
2. To feel comfortable and nonpressured.
3. To have your undivided attention.
4. For you not to judge their ability to buy whatever you're selling.
5. For you to focus more on them than on your work activities, rules, or schedules.
6. For you not to ignore them in favor of someone who you may think will buy more.

Customers are very sensitive and know whether or not you really care about them.

DAILY SUCCESS DIARY
ASK HOW TO HELP CUSTOMERS

You're learning to be customer-needs focused. An important objective, then, is to identify what their needs are. You understand needs by asking questions.

Practice the following action guides and you'll not only find out people's needs, but you'll also impress them with your sincerity.

	S	M	T	W	TH	F	S
Ask How to Help Customers							
1. Ask, "How may I help you?"							
2. Find out why they came in or contacted you.							
3. Ask open-ended questions to further understand their needs.							
Total each day							
Daily average per week							

Chapter 4

LISTEN
TO CUSTOMERS

"PLEASE LISTEN
TO ME AND
UNDERSTAND ME!"

When you get good at listening to people you'll tower above others who try to get your customers' money.

After you carefully *ask* how you can help people, it's time to do something that very few people do well—*listen!*

And don't just listen casually; rather, tune in to each person, cut out your own distractions, and really listen to what they tell you. Listen to their words, sure; but more important, listen to their tone of voice and body language.

You probably already listen well, but to learn a valuable lesson all you have to do is observe the next six people from whom you try to buy something. Watch how they listen to you. Notice how interested they are in you. See if they genuinely try to understand your needs.

Recently, I went into Brooks Brothers in Dallas to look at some suits. It was July and they still had tropical-weight dark suits. I live in Phoenix and can wear tropical-weight suits year around, but stores in Phoenix don't carry dark-colored traditional ones.

A very attractive young woman approached me and automatically assumed I was telling the truth when I replied, "I'm just looking," so she left me alone to wander around through the suit section. I tried to get her attention a couple of times but couldn't so I walked out. I was secretly wishing that she had tried to sell me something, or at least asked enough questions to know that I was really serious.

In about a half hour I went back in. She saw me and I suppose thought that I was still "just looking" because she didn't even approach me.

Now, as I said, she was attractive and had a professional appearance. I could tell that she was a bright, sharp person.

It was only after I pulled three suits out and looked at them under a light and had given her signals that I needed help by looking directly at her that she came over and again asked if she could help me.

She told me that the suits I was looking at were machine-made and that the store had some that were much better quality. I asked to see them and pulled out a navy one and a charcoal-gray one and asked if I could try them on.

She assumed that I was going to choose one of the two and was surprised when I told her, after trying them on, that I would take both.

To this point she'd asked me no questions. She didn't know *who* I was, *where* I lived, *why* I came into her store, *what* my work is, *where* I wanted to wear the suits, or *why* I wanted those colors.

Nor did she suggest shirts, ties, or any other items that might coordinate with the suits.

While she was processing my American Express card and writing down the shipping information, I watched her carefully to see how she would handle everything.

My conclusion was here was an attractive, bright, intelligent person with a bit of a sense of humor. A person whose character and qualities would impress a manager who was hiring people—but who had not been properly trained in the skills of customer-needs-focused selling.

She didn't ask questions that would tell her my needs. Nor did she really listen to me and try to understand my needs.

Clearly, she was product-focused, not customer-needs focused.

She thought she was selling clothing. She didn't view her job as helping people look better, feel better, appear more professional, or get better value in their clothing selections.

She didn't know that she was in business to give end-result benefits to customers, not just to sell clothing. I secretly wished she would have found out *what* I do, *why* I wanted the suits and *how* I planned to wear them. I would have reacted more positively if she had said, "Oh, so you conduct seminars for companies. Well let me help you make the strongest professional appearance."

But she didn't do that. She didn't know that I didn't want the suits just to have suits, but that I wanted them for specific end-result benefits.

Giving end-result benefits to customers begins by knowing what end-result benefits people want. And that can happen only when we *ask questions* and *listen*.

In this chapter we'll not only think of listening but we'll specifically break it down into these three dimensions:

1. Listen to words.
2. Listen to tone of voice.
3. Listen to body language.

HOW TO DO TOTAL LISTENING

Listening isn't just *hearing*. It's also *understanding*. It's understanding feelings and emotions. It's picking up subtle voice inflections and meanings. It's observing what people do with their hands and eyes—the congruence of their body language with their words.

In the Brooks Brothers store my words said, "I'm just looking." My body language said, "I'm interested in buying."

She didn't hear me, because she listened only to my words.

I still remember a facilitator training seminar I conducted in 1970. One of the participants was a speech professor at a university. We were talking about interpersonal communications—specifically listening. He made a comment that I'll never forget. He said, "Each person we meet has a common need—for us to listen to how they *feel*!"

"To listen to how they *feel*?" I repeated to myself silently. "Feel?"

I was struck with his choice of words.

It dawned upon me that although I may unconsciously listen to how people feel—I'd always called it empathy—I didn't consciously do it. I didn't do it automatically.

I've thought of his words many times. They've helped me learn to listen to people's *emotions*, not just their *words*.

They've helped me do total listening. It changed the way I communicate with people. It was a great lesson for me.

Breaking PREOCCUPATION

What gets in our way of effective listening? Mainly preoccupation.

Preoccupation is thinking about something else while I'm supposed to be listening to you. It's allowing my own feelings, biases, or problems to occupy my thoughts, and screening out what people tell me. While this is quite normal for all of us, our customers—people who pay us money— have a right to our undivided attention.

But I didn't get the undivided attention of the cashier at a car wash last week. She was obviously talking to her boyfriend, and apparently thought that if she didn't look me in my eyes, I'd go away and not bother her.

It became quite clear to me that I wasn't at the top on her priority list.

Now, someone might say, "Oh come on, that's no big deal...she's only a minimum wage person anyway."

Well, she may have been a minimum-wage person, but I'm not. I'm a $650-a-year person to that car wash—or another one. It's funny, but I can't remember the quality of the wash job. I assume it was OK. But I do remember the cashier. That's what I specifically remember about my experience.

That same day I went into a Laura Ashley shop to look for a gift for each of my daughters. The clerk was friendly and, sensing that I was like a fish out of water, became very interested and helpful. She asked several questions, made me feel comfortable in my ignorance, and gave some suggestions that showed her interest and concern. Sensing my fear of buying the wrong style or size, she reassured me and helped me feel comfortable.

What impressed me was that she had no preoccupation, she wasn't looking over my shoulder to see who else she could be selling to. She looked into my eyes. She listened because she seemed to care about helping me. She had me describe each of my daughters and then talked about them as if they were her friends.

She really listened.

So did Donna M. Jackson of Newton Manufacturing Company of Newton, Iowa. Donna, a graduate of our *customer* program, writes:

> When I am on the phone, I take time to picture the person I'm talking to and listen intently to what they're saying...

I still struggle with giving them my undivided attention. When there are so many things that need to be done it takes discipline to listen to the caller and just let my other work wait.

I find that I can find solutions much faster by listening closer.

Another graduate, Kim Shepard, who works in the gift shop aboard the SS *Norway* cruise ship, writes:

I've worked in retailing for eleven years and am always happy to learn such positive information. I have improved my ability to listen to my customers. Letting them talk the majority of the time has improved my sales and attitudes toward my customers.

There are many rewards for us as we develop the skill of breaking our preoccupation and really listening to people.

Drifting eyes mean a drifting mind

When you buy something from someone watch what that person does with his or her eyes and hands.

People often say the right words, but their eyes lack congruence and betray their true feelings or attention. Like the old song, "Your lips tell me 'yes, yes,' but there's 'no, no' in your heart." Hey, don't laugh, I told you the song was old!

People who are really listening to you look into your eyes. Said another way, when people aren't looking into your eyes, it's virtually impossible for them to hear everything you're trying to tell them. Said yet another way, when people are preoccupied, they almost never keep total eye contact.

Said still another way, when you force direct eye contact you'll not be preoccupied.

Eye contact is something that you can train yourself to do. Constantly do it with each customer, patient, guest, or client for twenty-one days and you'll develop a habit so strong that you'll then do it unconsciously. It'll be a natural part of your communication skills.

Many years ago someone taught me to look into just *one* of another person's eyes when I listened to them. That person pointed out, and I believe it, that when we do this we just naturally make a stronger impact upon them than we'd do otherwise.

Makes sense, doesn't it?

When you have this focused eye contact you concentrate all your emotional energy upon people. Doing this automatically causes a break in preoccupation.

Not only will this focused eye contact make a stronger impact upon people, it'll also help you communicate your sincere desire to understand their needs and serve them better.

And they'll know it too! They'll get the message that you're someone special.

Another benefit of concentrated eye contact is that it helps you listen much more effectively to customers. It causes you to understand them better and to communicate your sincere desire to help them.

Customers *intuitively* respect people more who look them in their eyes. All this happens on deep, emotional, unconscious levels.

Another way to better understand what people are telling us is to watch their hands as they talk and listen.

What do people do with their hands when they talk? What do they do when they're listening? Answering these questions can help you understand people much more effectively.

Let's think for a moment what people's hands tell us.

First, people will usually exhibit either closed or open gestures. Open gestures usually reveal that they're positive, that they trust you, feel comfortable with you and are allowing you to get through to them.

Closed gestures often mean that people are protecting themselves from you, carefully screening you out or assessing you. It may also mean that they're uncomfortable in a buying situation.

People show open gestures by widening their arms when they talk. By smiles and laughs. By moving in close to you. By nodding affirmatively. By opening their palms to you when they talk. By keeping their hands away from their mouths when they talk.

They show closed gestures when they fold their arms. When they cover their mouths as they talk. When they're constantly moving away from you. When they stare to the right or left of your head, rather than looking directly into your eyes. When they clutch purses or briefcases tightly to their bodies.

Watching their gestures is another dimension of listening.

PEOPLE OFTEN MIRROR THE BODY LANGUAGE YOU MODEL

Want to have some fun with an experiment that will help you learn something you'll never forget?

Next time you're around someone (not customers), regardless of what they're doing with their arms, tightly fold yours. Then watch what they do. The odds are 3 to 1 that they'll mirror you and unconsciously fold theirs. Then unfold yours and show open gestures and see how quickly they do the same.

And then, the next time you're in a group of people, when everyone is comfortable, force a yawn several times within a couple of minutes. After you do, look around and see what the others are doing. I'll guarantee you that several will begin to yawn.

They will...because people unconsciously tend to copy or mirror the body language we model.

What this means is that once you decide on the positive responses you want to *get* from people, you can get them by *modeling* the same positive behavior to them.

Specifically, your positive, open body language will cause many of your customers to adopt the same kind.

So, what's all this got to do with *listening*?

Everything!

Listening isn't just hearing the words people say, it's also understanding how they feel. It's sensing how open they are to you. It's understanding tone of voice and body language. It's emotionally plugging into them.

LISTENING IS THE HIGHEST FORM OF PERSUASION

There's probably no better way to persuade your customers—to get them to believe you, have confidence in you, and buy from you—than to truly listen to them.

Listening is just about the most powerful form of persuasion.

When you listen you silently say to your customers, "I want to understand you; I want to understand your needs or wants; I want to solve your problems, because you're important, and I know that when you're happy and satisfied, you'll come back and tell others. Then I'll be more successful."

When you have this attitude you'll persuade people in a powerful way.

IN SUMMARY

Few people listen well. Check it out the next time you go to buy something, or have a problem.

You'll make strong, positive impressions on people when you truly listen to them.

The secret is to do *total* listening. To break your own preoccupation by tuning your world out and tuning customers in. To refrain from interrupting people. To remove biases that filter out what people say.

When communicating with people, develop the habit of looking into just *one* of their eyes. This keeps you from being distracted. It plugs you into them and guarantees against your preoccupation.

Notice where people put their eyes when they talk and when they listen. This will help you establish rapport and better understand them.

Be conscious of your own body language. Show open gestures that prove you're listening.

Read this chapter over and over and practice the ideas in it. You'll develop more confidence with people, and they'll notice and feel better about you.

And you'll notice your persuasive skills increase immediately.

HOW TO GET GOOD AT LISTENING TO CUSTOMERS

1. Listen to people's words.
2. Listen to their tone of voice.
3. Listen to their body language.

SOMETHING TO THINK ABOUT

According to Dr. Albert Mahrabian, a UCLA professor, communication effectiveness consists of:

1. 7% verbal
2. 38% tone of voice
3. 55% nonverbal—body language

EVALUATING YOUR LISTENING SKILLS

Want to check out your listening skills after each of your contacts with people? Want to have a clear understanding about how much you really hear, observe, and remember?

Take a few minutes twice each day, just after contact with one or more persons, and assess yourself. Ask these questions and see if you can answer them.

1. What color were the persons' eyes?
2. What did they do with their hands?
3. How comfortable were they with you?
4. How effective were your questions in drawing them out?
5. How well did you understand what they were wanting or looking for?
6. What distinctly unique features did you remember about them?
7. Did you remember their names?
8. Could you call their names and recognize them again?
9. If they called you on the phone would you remember them?
10. If they described you to another person, how would you want them to do it?

Answer the preceding questions, in light of what you're learning in this book, and you'll do a great job listening.

All this will help you plug into your customers' real feelings and needs.

DAILY SUCCESS DIARY
LISTEN TO CUSTOMERS

Few things will impress people more than tuning the world out and listening to them. Listening is the most powerful form of persuasion.

As you practice the following action guides, you'll better understand people, and your persuasive skills will increase.

	S	M	T	W	TH	F	S
Listen To Customers							
1. Listen to words							
2. Listen to tone of voice							
3. Listen to body language							
Total each day							
Daily average per week							

Chapter 5

HELP
CUSTOMERS

"HELP ME GET
WHAT I WANT!"

So far in this book you're seeing a customer-service system emerge. Let's take a moment and look back where we've been.

You've learned to first *greet* and gain rapport with people when you come into contact with them. You understood that a lot of selling takes place the first few minutes of contact—whether in person or over the telephone.

Next, you learned to *value* customers—to think of them as important people who pay your salary.

Third, you learned to *ask* how you can help people. You discovered how to ask open-ended questions to find out why they came in or contacted you, or what they want that you can help them enjoy.

Then I shared how to *listen* to customers—to tune the world out and understand what people say with their words, tone of voice, and body language.

All these steps will help you put people at ease, show your sincerity, and find out their needs. They prepare you to help customers by first understanding what they want.

PRODUCT-FOCUSED OR CUSTOMER-NEEDS FOCUSED?

In today's competitive marketplace the leaders who emerge successfully will be people who are customer-needs focused. Because they have more choices of what and from whom they buy, people who pay you money for products or services are demanding more. And they have a right to do this. After all, it's their money.

In order to compete, organizations are discovering that they must become customer-needs focused.

What does it mean to be customer-needs focused, rather than product focused?

Well, to explain, let me paint two scenes—each illustrating a specific focus.

Greg and Allison, both in their mid-twenties, gazing into each other's eyes, went into two jewelry stores looking for an engagement ring.

In the first store they entered they received a pleasant greeting and a "May I help you?" from a nice person.

"We're really just looking," they told the salesperson, but they walked directly to the case that held the diamonds.

Knowing the business, as well as not missing the body language and silent excitement of the couple, the salesperson remarked, "We have a special promotion on diamonds today..."

At this point he began to flood the couple with information about why his store's diamonds are such a good buy. He talked about how their diamonds are carefully selected, as well as the quality of their mountings. He also extolled his company's great reputation.

Then, sensing the price range that the couple would probably want based on their appearance and age, the salesperson unlocked the case and pulled out one ring and showed it to the couple.

When they reacted with uncertainty, the salesperson then put it back, and one by one, showed them several rings. Each time he did, he flooded them with product information—facets, cut, color, clarity, and so forth.

With all this information, the couple got confused and told the man that they'd have to think it over and that they wanted to look around.

Hearing this for the ten-thousandth time, he smiled and mentally dismissed them as not being serious prospects.

Then Greg and Allison went to another store that has thoroughly trained its people in customer-needs, focused-selling skills.

A nice, friendly salesperson greeted them and sincerely thanked them for coming in. Instantly, they felt comfortable—not so much from the saleswoman's words, but from her manner and attitude toward them.

"*How* may I help you?" she asked.

"We're really just kinda looking," Allison responded, and together they walked directly to the diamonds.

"Well," the salesperson smiled broadly, "please make yourselves comfortable, and...just let me know of anything I can explain to you."

The salesperson smiled and put them at ease, taking the pressure off them. Then she added, "Is there a special occasion?"

Having asked this, she didn't need to hear a verbal response—she got her answer in the broad smile each of them gave as they squeezed the other's hand and blushed a bit.

"Well, we *are* getting engaged...and, well, we're looking for a ring..."

"That's wonderful," the salesperson smiled at them. "When's the occasion?"

"July the 17th," came their happy reply.

To this the salesperson exclaimed her excitement and very sensitively asked some questions. Not direct questions like, "What are you looking for?" She asked more indirect ones.

In the next few minutes this alert salesperson found out all this information:

When they met
What they do
Where they went to school
Where their parents live
What their parents do
What fears they have about this purchase
How much they were prepared to spend
When they planned to make a purchase decision

She asked them several questions that they had never even thought to ask themselves. She understood their dominant buying motives, as well as the size stone and design of mounting they wanted.

All this information was professionally gathered in a very conversational, nonaggressive way.

After understanding what they wanted she put them further at ease by saying, "Well, the reason I'm asking you so many questions is that I'm not interested in just selling you a ring. Rather, I want to help you select the very best value and make sure you get a ring that you'll be proud of for years to come.

"Let me show you," she went on, "a ring that will look beautiful on you and will be an excellent value."

She then showed them a ring and emphasized the beauty, clarity, and value that it would give them.

Notice how the first salesperson was product focused. He thought he was selling jewelry. He assumed that people would buy when they knew all about the product features.

The second one knew better. She knew that people don't buy diamond rings just because of the price or size; rather they buy because of the beauty, how it will look on them, as well as the emotions and commitment it symbolizes.

Now here's my point. People don't buy your products or services for what they are, but for what they'll *do* for them. They buy for the end-result benefits they'll enjoy.

This sounds so simple, but most people who work with customers don't know it. At least they don't practice it. Go shop three stores and check me out if you don't believe me.

How to help customers

Whatever you're selling or whatever you do for customers, you'll help them better when you focus on the following three suggestions:

1. Satisfy their wants or needs.
2. Solve their problems.
3. Give them extra value.

Satisfy their wants or needs

Remember, people don't buy products or services just to have the products or services; they buy to satisfy needs they want filled, desires they want satisfied, or problems they want solved.

Here are some of the reasons why people buy things:

To be entertained

To receive pleasure

To enjoy peace of mind

To receive recognition

To economize or save money

To impress others

To have better health

To promote friendships or family togetherness

To gratify their own egos

To prevent future losses

To acquire or possess

These wants or needs become *reasons* why people buy—dominant buying motives. Understanding them helps you become more successful.

I learned a great lesson about this recently at a supermarket in Houston, Texas.

A supermarket is a supermarket is a supermarket. Right?

Well, maybe it is in your city, but not in Houston, Texas, at Randalls.

Randalls is definitely different—unique in display, layout, and atmosphere. But where it really smacks you is in customer service.

"What makes Randalls different from other supermarkets?" I asked Jeff Savage, a store manager.

"We'll do anything to please a customer," he quickly responded.

"Anything?" I asked suspiciously, thinking it sounded like an exaggeration.

"Yeah, anything," he shot back.

"To what limit will you *not* go?" I asked, getting down to business quickly.

"There are *no* limits," he replied, giving me the distinct feeling that he had been asked that question before.

Just then a man came up with a turkey and told Jeff that it was "rancid." Then, while the man fished for his cash register receipt to prove he'd bought the turkey there, Jeff, quickly relieving the man from any need to explain, told him, "Well, let's get you another one...and allow me to apologize to you for your inconvenience. Tomorrow is one day [Thanksgiving] that you need to get a good turkey!"

Taken back at the ease of it all, the man tried to show Jeff his receipt. "Hey, no problem, I trust you," Jeff responded, not even looking at the receipt, and asked a clerk standing by to let the customer select his choice of any size turkey. The customer's not-so-thrilled-at-having-to-return-the-turkey attitude was quickly transformed into one of surprise and appreciation.

"What is the most blatant, unmerited request a customer has ever asked you?" I asked Jeff as the man with the turkey left.

He eyed me as if to say, "I don't understand the question." So I repeated it.

"I don't think in terms of customers being blatant or wrong, I just think in terms of pleasing them," he replied.

"We will get anything for anyone. We recently sent a man to California to find an item that we had requests to get. About every month I special order a case of Campbell's split pea soup for one of our customers. We don't stock it, but I personally special order it and then call her when it comes in."

Well, there's much more to the Randalls story and to their total commitment to customer service. It was a joy to visit them and to see that a supermarket doesn't have to be just a supermarket. It can be a most pleasurable experience when it has a total customer focus.

SOLVE THEIR PROBLEMS

The managers and employees at Randalls also see themselves as problem solvers. This might be a good way for you to look at what you do.

A man who was an office manager in a retail furniture business once enrolled in one of my classes. When I first asked him what he did he replied, "I help people solve their problems.

"Someone told me many years ago," he went on, "that I'd always get paid consistent with the size problems I helped people solve.

"So," he concluded, "ever since then I've seen myself as a problem solver."

What kinds of problems do *you* help people solve?

Later in this book I'll give you a four-step problem-solving formula that can help you serve your customers better so they'll pay you more.

GIVE THEM EXTRA VALUE

I often ask managers and employees of firms this question, "What do you give customers that they can't get elsewhere?"

It's an important question that, when asked and answered, can help put you ahead of competitors.

So, let me ask *you*...what do *you* give people that they can't get elsewhere? What do *you* do for customers that your competitors don't?

As I said, it's an incredibly important question.

I ask it of many people. When I recently asked it of a dentist who was in a seminar I was conducting, I got a most surprising response. Read carefully; there's a great lesson to be learned.

Visiting a dental office isn't at the top of most people's list of memorable experiences, is it?

But then, most people have never been to see Dr. Ron Bentham of Country Pines Dental Centre in Penticton, British Columbia.

Ron Bentham's dental office is, well, not exactly like most other dental offices you've visited.

For starters, it looks like a comfortable home as you drive up to it. Upon entering, you walk into, not a typical waiting/reception room, but a giant country kitchen complete with a harvest table, chairs, and colonial William Bradford upholstered chairs.

The beautiful colors and tasteful appointments make a very pleasing visual appearance, but the most impressive sensory impression is yet to come. Patients are greeted with, not the typical smells of a dental office, but with the pleasant aroma of freshly baked muffins. Yeah, muffins! Upon entering, each person is offered one of these wonderfully smelling delicacies. The menu changes daily—blueberry one day, applesauce the next, and so on.

Patients are also offered them when they leave the office. Needless to say, they leave with a lasting impression of their visit to the dental office.

But that's not all. Dr. Bentham also has fresh-cut flowers in the reception room each day. Most of the people receive a flower when they leave. He offers a pick-up service for senior citizens. On their way home his driver will even stop by the supermarket or other places where his patients need to shop.

Now you may be thinking, "Well, all that sounds nice, but it sounds much too extravagant." Of course, it does cost a bit extra to add these touches, yet with a staff of five people his revenues are *three times* what traditional dental offices ring up.

So convinced is he that excellent customer service is the key to even greater success, he's constantly looking for ways to improve his staff's quality and quantity of patient care. He takes them to seminars and programs and consistently looks for other creative ways to differentiate his office. His goal is to give his patients the most pleasant, memorable *experience* possible.

Other dental offices accuse him of unfair competition, saying that his methods are actually "marketing" and unprofessional.

He smiles all the way to the bank, and his happy patients flaunt their beautiful new smiles all around town. Then, when they remember those delicious hot muffins, fresh-cut flowers, and friendly staff, they smile as they look forward to their next visit to his office.

Viewing What You Do As A Partnership

The term "Partnering" is frequently being used to describe the relationship between sellers and buyers. It suggests a value-focused relationship. It brings a whole new dimension of trust between organizations and their customers, and just as important, it brings greater satisfaction and levels of confidence to both sides.

Here's an excerpt from a letter from Jim Vogeley, president of a company in Newport News, Virginia, called nView.

> Your program has successfully convinced my people that a customer/supplier relationship is not a "we versus they" sort

of thing, but rather a partnership where the customer and supplier are working together to solve a problem or need.

Working under this new-found attitude, I believe that our people are performing their customer-service duties more efficiently and that they are leaving customers with a warm feeling about our company.

Equally important, they have a better attitude about their jobs and are much more relaxed when working with customers.

Yes, partnering with customers or working together with them to solve their problems or fill their needs, while not only the way to do business in the future, also adds much more meaning to what we do.

IN SUMMARY

When you've *greeted* customers, *valued* them, *asked* how you can help them, and *listened* to them so you understand their needs, it's now time to *help* them fill their needs.

In doing this, just realize that people don't buy your product or service for what it *is*, but for what it will *do* for them. People buy for end-result benefits.

The end-result benefits are what your product or service will do for people, how it will help them, how it will cause them to look good to others, and other buying motives.

As you *help* people, avoid being product focused, but be customer-needs focused. Center your communication around how customers will benefit, not around the product or service features.

Again, don't just tell people what your product or service *is*, but dwell on how it will help them enjoy end-result benefits.

Study and understand the principles in this chapter and you'll quickly be noticed by your customers. They'll know that you're not just trying to sell them something, but are sincerely helping them fill their wants or needs.

HOW TO GET GOOD AT HELPING CUSTOMERS

1. Satisfy their wants or needs.
2. Solve their problems.
3. Give them extra value.

SOMETHING TO THINK ABOUT

To remain competitive today, businesses and professions must change from a product or service focus to a customer-needs focus.

ELEVATING YOURSELF ABOVE YOUR COMPETITORS

Your unique factors can cause you to stick out in the minds of your customers. Unique factors are creative things you do that customers aren't expecting.

Creative activities aren't always easy to think of. That's why most people don't do them. They aren't willing or aren't challenged to think them up.

This exercise isn't easy, but you can do it if you want to. All you have to do is ask and answer the following questions.

"What do I give customers that they can't get elsewhere?"

"What can I say, or what can I give customers that will cause them to remember me?"

"What can I do to followup and thank people even when they don't buy from me?"

"What extra value can I give people *after* they buy from me?"

"What can I give customers that will be totally unexpected?"

How did you answer these questions? What actions will you take? What are your expected results?

DAILY SUCCESS DIARY
HELP CUSTOMERS

Your attentiveness and conscientiousness in helping people satisfy their wants or needs elevates you above others with whom they deal. It's your attitude that sets you apart.

This week, review this chapter several times and focus on the action guides.

	S	M	T	W	TH	F	S
Help Customers							
1. Satisfy their wants or needs							
2. Solve their problems							
3. Give them extra value							
Total each day							
Daily average per week							

Chapter 6

INVITE CUSTOMERS BACK

"LET ME KNOW THAT I'M WELCOME BACK ANYTIME!"

What can you do to cause your customers, patients, members, or guests to want to continue to do business with you?

What can you do that sticks out in their minds and makes them want to come back to see you, contact you again, continue to give you their money?

When you answer this question carefully, then follow up with action, you'll leave each customer with positive feelings about his or her experience with you.

Just as *first* impressions are memorable, so are *last* impressions. People carry their feelings with them when they *leave* you, and this impacts their choices the next time they need your products or services.

How DO YOU WANT CUSTOMERS TO FEEL AFTER CONTACT WITH YOU?

How *do* you want people to feel after they've had contact with you—either in person or over the telephone? What do you want them to say about you? How do you want them to describe their experience?

In seminars I often ask participants to answer these questions:

1. How do you want people to feel after having contact with you?
2. What do you want them to say about you?

3. How do you want them to describe their experience with you?

Stop reading a moment, take out a sheet of paper, and write your responses to these three questions. Making yourself write down answers will also cause you to think. This activity forces answers that won't occur to you if you only read them.

Please, stop reading and take a few moments to write down your responses.

Not long ago I was conducting a seminar for dentists and dental assistants. We had spent time writing down mission statements—statements that defined the purpose of what they do and the value they give patients.

After they wrote mission statements I asked them to write out *exit statements*. I asked them to visualize an impartial person standing outside their entrance asking each patient who leaves this question, "How would you describe the treatment experience you've just had?"

"If someone did ask that question to each of your patients as they leave," I went on, "exactly what would you want their responses to be?"

Then I handed index cards to the participants and asked them to write their responses.

This exercise caused them to face a sobering reality. It made them think in new dimensions. They concluded, "If I want patients to feel a certain way after leaving, I can insure that feeling by the treatment I give them when they're here."

Immediately, their enthusiasm increased, as did the way they handled people during contact. Their objectives, or mission to help patients enjoy the very best treatment experience, influenced their actions and behavior when with them.

How to Make the Best Last Impressions

We talk a lot about making the best *first* impressions. Now let's run ahead and think about making the best *last* impressions. In order to make the best last impressions, here are three action guides to follow:

1. Thank people for coming in or contacting you.
2. Ask them to return soon.
3. Leave them wanting to return.

Practicing these action guides will cause you to appear professional and leave people feeling good about their contact with you.

Thank People for Coming in or Contacting You

This can be done with words, actions, or attitudes. Expressing appreciation first begins with sincere attitudes and values. If you are truly appreciative, you'll communicate it, whether you do it verbally or nonverbally.

You should always cheerfully express your appreciation whether people buy from you or not. This positive disposition sets the stage for future success and referrals.

I heard a great example of this recently. You'll enjoy hearing it.

A man came into the Lexus of Brookfield dealership in suburban Milwaukee, Wisconsin, with three bottles of champagne to give to the general manager, Jim Johnson, and two employees.

Yes, champagne! To a car dealership's employees! See...I told you that you wouldn't believe it.

The man had neither bought a car there, nor had he ever had his car serviced there. So why would he bring in three bottles of bubbly to give them?

It all started when his car, which he had purchased at another dealership, stalled out a couple of blocks from the Lexus of Brookfield dealership. Leaving it by the side of the road, he walked down to their dealership to ask to use their phone.

Now, get the picture...here's someone going into a car dealership to ask a favor rather than looking to buy something. We'd immediately figure that this guy would be as welcome as a flu bug in a surgical ward. But not in this case...as you'll soon see.

Explaining that his car had stalled out two blocks away, the man was surprised that the salesperson showed unusual concern. The salesperson asked him what kind of car he had and what had happened to cause it to stall. Then, rather than just showing him the telephone and allowing him to use it while he waited for someone who had money to spend, the salesperson asked what dealership he had purchased the car from.

The man had bought it from a Toyota dealer whose competition, another Toyota dealership, was owned by the same man who owned the Lexus dealership.

Finding out this information, the salesperson helped get the car towed to the dealership where the man had purchased it. He then personally drove the man to the dealership and went in with him to make sure he got helped. He got the man's name and called him back that evening to make sure everything went all right. He did all this with no other motive than to help the man who wasn't even a customer.

Now that's service!

Hearing about this, and being in Milwaukee, I went in and interviewed Jim Johnson, who confirmed the story.

He then explained to me their commitment to total customer satisfaction. He told me their values and rules of employee conduct, as well as their objective of doing the right thing in all their dealings. He told me they routinely send one dozen long-stemmed roses to each customer who buys a car from them.

He also proudly mentioned that their dealership had a strong shot at being number one in Lexus' Customer Satisfaction Index in the whole nation that year. And, oh yes, they enjoy excellent profitability.

After listening to him, I understood why the man brought him the three bottles of champagne.

The next time this person thought of buying a car, or whenever a friend thought of buying one, where do you think he'll go?

Jim also told an unusual story of a couple purchasing a Lexus from them and then referring over a dozen other people to their dealership.

What made it unusual was that one day this couple came in looking at his cars, saying that they couldn't afford one, but if they could they'd buy a Lexus from him. They were a nice young couple with stars in their eyes, clearly in love with his vehicles. Later they called him and told him that although they couldn't afford to purchase a vehicle, their anniversary was coming up and they'd scraped their money together and wanted to rent a car for the weekend.

Jim explained that they didn't rent cars. But sensing the couple's excitement, said, "While we don't rent cars, I will loan you my demonstrator for three days as my anniversary gift to you!"

And he did!

They were bowled over. No, blown away is a more apt description.

A year later they came in and purchased a Lexus, and as I mentioned earlier, referred over a dozen people to him.

"Pretty dumb of him to do something like that!" skeptics may say. But was it? To reach a conclusion, all you have to do is look at the reputation and profitability he enjoys to see that it was a pretty smart thing to do.

It would be interesting to know just how many cars he sells in the next five years because he acted in a professional manner and caused these people to want to come back.

He knows the value of leaving people feeling good about going into his dealership.

Ask them to return soon

One reason why people love you to show appreciation to them is because it's so uncommon!

Think this accusation is unfair? Just notice the attitudes of people who serve or sell you. Even when you purchase something, they don't always leave you wanting to return. Just let them get the idea that you aren't going to buy anything and you'll usually get abandoned.

The restaurant hostess, bank teller, sales clerk, or dental receptionist who takes the time to say "Thank you for choosing us…and please return soon" makes a strong impact on us.

One of my all-time favorite restaurants is La Dolce Vita in Beverly Hills, just between where Wilshire Boulevard crosses Santa Monica Boulevard. I've been going there since

1969 and never miss a chance to eat there whenever I'm in the area.

One of the owners, Jimmy or George, was always there to greet me and welcome me. It was nice to be remembered. Each time, when I left, they'd ask, "When are you coming back to California again?"

I always left feeling good and wanting to return. The last time I was there George had passed on and Jimmy was out, but his son was at the front door of the small restaurant. He was just as friendly.

I have probably eaten there thirty to forty times—all because of the good food, better service, and even better first and last impressions. Each time they made me want to come back.

They never failed to *ask*.

LEAVE THEM WANTING TO RETURN.

When customer-centered *attitudes* and *values* are shown through our *actions* customers will have good feelings and memories about us. When our attitudes and values are right, our actions will usually be right.

The whole buying, shopping, treatment, or service experience plants positive or negative feelings within customers, and this whole experience either causes them to want or not to want to come back.

See if you'd want to go back to this shop.

I walked out of a hotel in Minneapolis and saw a hand-printed sign in the window of a cigar store. It said, "No change made!"

Curious, I went in and asked the attendant what the sign meant. Eyeing me suspiciously, he growled through his cigar, "If I didn't have that sign there, people would bother me all day asking for parking meter change."

"Yeah, well, you certainly wouldn't want that to happen," I thought to myself, as I left his shop.

I can still remember thinking, "Hey, man, if I owned that shop I'd put a sign in the window that said, 'Change made with a smile.'"

In fact, as I looked at the small number of parking meters close by I visualized myself watching them and personally putting a nickel or a dime in them with a note attached to the driver's wiper blade that said, "When you park close to my store I'll even try to watch your meter for you. Thanks for referring me to your friends."

This experience became sort of a metaphor for me, and since then I've noticed the same attitude in many businesses. With their actions they clearly say, "No change made here! Don't bother us unless you want to buy something!" Or they say, "And don't ask for any special favors either!"

Sadly, in these competitive times many of these organizations aren't in business any longer. The ones that are still around will find slimmer chances for survival in the years ahead, as customers demand the high level of service they deserve.

Customers *are* becoming more demanding, which, of course, they have a right to be. They have more choices as to what they buy and from whom they buy. This presents a gloomy future for some organizations—ones who don't focus on customers' needs. But it spells "insurmountable opportunities" for those wide-awake firms who have shifted to a true customer focus.

One way to cause customers to remember you favorably is to do something that's totally unexpected and out of the ordinary. Simple actions are most memorable—a small, chewy chocolate for your restaurant guest, a genuine "thank you" just before your customer leaves, an inexpensive gift, a thank-you note. Be different; use your imagination.

Businesses that thrive in the future will be ones that say, "Bother me even if you don't want to buy anything!" Or, "Ask for special favors and just see how fast I give them to you!"

Be creative and send a silent, clear message with your actions, "Change enthusiastically made here!"

DO SOMETHING THAT STICKS IN YOUR CUSTOMERS' MINDS

In almost every business or profession there's something you can do that leaves people with an unexpected feeling of joy. The secret is to do something *unexpected.*

Dr. Bill Gregg and staff in El Toro, California, give their patients a toothbrush. Now, that's nice, but not totally unexpected. Then, before the patients leave their office they give them a piece of sugarless candy.

Dr. Ron Bentham of Penticton, B.C., not only offers his patients a hot muffin when they come in; his well-trained staff also offers to wrap up some muffins for them to take home.

Again, do something unexpected.

Doubletree Hotels give guests a giant chocolate chip cookie. Eat one and you'll kill for another. Now, since most of us aren't into killing, the next best thing to do is to go back and stay in a Doubletree Hotel.

The Ritz-Carlton Hotels have probably the best customer service and training of any hotel chain. Their credo is:

The Ritz-Carlton Hotel is a place where the genuine care and comfort of our guests is our highest mission.

We pledge to provide the finest personal service and facilities for our guests, who will always enjoy a warm, relaxed yet refined ambience.

The Ritz-Carlton experience enlivens the senses, instills well-being, and fulfills even the unexpressed wishes and needs of our guests.

One very important step that they recognize and instill in their people is, "A fond farewell." They drill their people to remember to, "Give them a warm good-bye and use their names, if and when possible."

Leave one of their hotels and, from the cashier to the person who smiles and closes your car door, you'll be made to feel very special. And you'll want to go back. The high level of service you enjoy there will stick in your mind as a permanent memory.

CUSTOMER SATISFACTION IS INFLUENCED BY OUR PEOPLE SKILLS

When people have contact with you, whether it's in person or over the telephone, their satisfaction will be greatly influenced by your people skills—your ability to relate to them in a positive manner. It also has a lot to do with your own self-esteem—how you see yourself and what you believe to be true about yourself.

Relating to building satisfaction in other employees, positive talk about your firm and its management all influence your self-esteem.

I see this growth all the time in our courses, which are conducted for hundreds of companies.

This was reinforced in a letter that I recently received from Celia Yancy, a training director in a Texas bank. She wrote:

> Your program develops and enhances those people skills (confidence, self-esteem, communication, courtesy, customer service, sales, team work, positive attitudes, etc.) that our association needs at this stage in our industry. If our employees don't feel confident, how can we expect our depositors to feel confident and remain with us? This is the foundation for taking us into the sales and service culture that will keep us competitive.
>
> It was amazing how many aspects of sales, customer service and courtesy were addressed and how new lines of communication opened up for peers with peers, managers with subordinates, and employees with customers.
>
> Attitudes—personally and professionally—had truly changed.

Success on the job, with other employees or with customers, does depend on our own self-esteem. It influences how we relate to people, how they feel about us, and how much customers will want to come back to see us.

IN SUMMARY

Successful businesses and organizations realize the need to invite customers, guests, or patients back. They know that this is a crucial step in causing long-term loyalty and satisfaction.

Getting good at inviting people back begins by identifying how you want them to feel after having contact with you. I'd strongly recommend that you design your own exit statement. This is a written statement of how you want customers to describe their experience with you.

Having an *exit statement* written down becomes a goal that helps influence your attitudes and actions when dealing with people.

Remember the importance of *last* impressions. Make sure the last impression you make on people is strong and positive. This will impact their desire to contact you again or refer their friends to you.

People go where they're appreciated—where they feel welcome and valued. And they return to offices, businesses, or organizations where they're invited back.

HOW TO GET GOOD AT INVITING CUSTOMERS BACK

1. Thank them for coming in or contacting you.
2. Ask them to return soon.
3. Leave them wanting to return.

SOMETHING TO THINK ABOUT

The last impression people have of you will stay with them until you have a chance to change it—if you ever have another chance!

GUARANTEEING YOUR FUTURE WITH CUSTOMERS

In most businesses or professions the real money is made in repeat business—sales that are made after the initial one has taken place.

Customers want to come back to see you or contact you again when they've had pleasant experiences—when they feel good about doing business with you.

So a major strategy for you is to insure your future with them.

Improvement begins with assessment and then action. Assess yourself in these areas:

1. Do I have a clear *exit statement* in mind?
   ( ) Yes( ) No
2. Do people call me back and thank me for helping them?
   ( ) Yes( ) No
3. Do most of my new customers come from old customer referrals?
   ( ) Yes( ) No
4. Does most of my current business come from old, satisfied customers?
   ( ) Yes( ) No
5. Do I have an ongoing process of keeping in touch with customers?
   ( ) Yes( ) No
6. Do I pay as much attention to people who don't buy from me as I do to ones who do?
   ( ) Yes( ) No

DAILY SUCCESS DIARY
INVITE CUSTOMERS BACK

People will remember their last impressions of you and be swayed by them whenever considering calling or contacting you again. So, you want their memory of you to be the best one possible.

Practice these action guides this week and score yourself each day.

	S	M	T	W	TH	F	S
Invite Customers Back							
1. Thank them for coming in or contacting you.							
2. Ask them to return soon.							
3. Leave them wanting to return.							
Total each day							
Daily average per week							

The Customer-Satisfaction System

1. *Greet* customers.
2. *Value* customers.
3. *Ask* how to help customers.
4. *Listen* to customers.
5. *Help* customers.
6. *Invite* customers back.

Chapter 7

THE CUSTOMER SATISFACTION SYSTEM

"EVERYTHING YOU NEED TO KNOW ABOUT SATISFYING ME!"

Well, in the last six chapters you have learned the six steps of the Customer-Satisfaction System. The six steps are:

1. *Greet* customers.
2. *Value* customers.
3. *Ask* how to help customers.
4. *Listen* to customers.
5. *Help* customers.
6. *Invite* customers back.

Now, I know that just because you read these six steps doesn't mean that you'll remember them...or that you'll *do* them. Frankly, in order to do them regularly, they must first become habits—automatic responses.

You'll want to learn this system so well that you do it unconsciously. This way you won't have to consciously think of doing it—each step will just pop into your mind when the occasion calls for it. You'll do it on autopilot—without thinking through each step—like when you tie your shoes or brush your teeth.

Doing it on autopilot is like when I ask, "9 times 9 equals what?" and you automatically answer, "81." Or, when I suggest, "Things go better with _____," you automatically respond, "Coke." You act from memory, as an automatic learned response, because the "answers" have been programmed into your memory by *repetition*. You can input the customer-satisfaction system the same way. You can *program* it into your *memory* by *repetition*.

"How can I do that?" you ask. "How can I memorize the system so I'll respond automatically in given situations?"

Read carefully.

Here's a memory-stacking method that'll take two minutes to learn, and then you'll always remember the six steps. So relax a bit and read carefully.

Ready?

OK, first visualize a giant *greeting* card, three feet high, standing open so you can see both inside panels. Get it? A giant greeting card that *greets* people.

Now mentally picture a gold bar of great *value* lying across the top of both panels of the greeting card.

Next, on the left side (as you're looking at it) of the gold bar of great *value* sits a pair of huge red wax lips that *ask* questions.

OK, let's stop for a moment and see where we are.

So far we have a giant three-foot *greeting* card, standing open, and a glittering gold bar of great *value* is lying across the top of the card. And sitting on the left side of the gold bar is a pair of huge red wax lips that *ask* questions.

Got it? Take just a moment and visualize these exaggerated objects.

Hey, hold on...don't close your mind on this. You may think this memory-stacking process is a little hokey, but just stick with me for two minutes and you'll see that you'll definitely remember it.

Let's go on.

On the right side of the gold bar of great *value* stands a big pink plastic ear that *listens*. The big pink plastic ear has a large mole on the upper part of it, with a black hair growing out of the mole. (Gross, huh?)

Next, standing with his right foot on the red wax lips that *ask* questions and his left foot in the pink plastic ear that *listens* is a suntanned hunk of a lifeguard who *helps* save people.

OK, now I know that some of you have already allowed your minds to wander and become distracted! Could I please have your attention again?

Look, if I'm going to single-handedly be responsible for your future fame and fortune, you're going to have to pay closer attention to me!

Now pick up your Crayolas and tidy up your desk.

OK, that's better.

And finally, stuck inside the top of our lifeguard's sunglasses is a wedding invitation that *invites* people.

Now, let's think through the picture again.

You have just visualized a giant greeting card that *greets* people. On top of it is a gold bar of great *value*. On the left side of the gold bar of great *value* is a pair of huge red wax lips that *ask* questions. On the right side of the gold bar of great *value* is a big pink plastic ear that *listens*. And standing with his right foot on the huge red wax lips that *ask* questions and his left foot on the big pink plastic ear that *listens*, is a suntanned hunk of a lifeguard who *helps* save people. Then finally, stuck behind the top of the lifeguard's sunglasses is a wedding invitation that *invites* people.

We have stacked up these illogical, exaggerated figures to remind you of these six steps.

1. *Greet* customers.
2. *Value* customers.
3. *Ask* how you can help customers.
4. *Listen* to customers.
5. *Help* customers.
6. *Invite* customers back.

You'll always remember these six steps.

Read this repetition carefully, see the exaggerated objects in your mind, and you'll always remember the giant greeting card that *greets* people, the huge red wax lips that *ask* questions, the big pink plastic ear with the mole, and the black hair growing out of it, that *listens*. You'll never forget the suntanned hunk of a lifeguard who *helps* people and the wedding invitation that *invites* people.

WHAT'S THE PAYOFF FOR YOU?

When you apply the Customer-Satisfaction System you'll enjoy many personal rewards as well as have more fun and success in your job.

The System will help you achieve a congruence between your actions and your own internal values. In short, you'll like yourself better.

Here's how a hair stylist at the Rusty Shear Haircutters in Phoenix felt better about herself as a result of learning and applying the System.

If stylists would realize that the only thing we have to offer our customers that they can't get somewhere else is better and more personal service!

When we learned to take all this to heart and look at things through the customer's point of view, customers became much more relaxed and felt much more welcome...

I have tripled my tips, my business has become easier and we are having record-breaking weeks because of your course.

Cliff Miller, an executive with A. A. Friedman Co. in Augusta, Georgia, wrote this about how learning this system helped his people.

> Our people don't just learn the material, they learn the *values* the material teaches. They feel better about their work because of this program.

> This has been accomplished by bringing our company's needs (to sell diamonds) into congruence with their values (to do something worthwhile). Consequently, our people perform better because they *want* to.

There is within each of us an inner need to be part of a worthwhile event. To see meaning to our work.

When we focus on creating value for others we plug ourselves into a congruence that causes us to like ourselves more, have more confidence, do better jobs, and create higher levels of customer satisfaction.

Well now, if you've read this chapter so far, something has happened to you. You've learned, and will *never* forget, the six-step Customer-Satisfaction System.

But just remembering it isn't enough. To really help you, you need to internalize the steps and automatically practice them at appropriate times. You must do them on autopilot.

Sound difficult? No, you'll be amazed at how simple this really is. And you'll also be surprised at how much confidence it gives you with people.

Here's all you have to do. For the next 21 days, twice each day, mentally rehearse the memory-stacking objects. Just visualize each object and say it to yourself. Just say, "A giant greeting card that *greets* people, a gold bar of great *value*, huge red wax lips that *ask* questions, a big pink plastic ear that *listens*, a suntanned hunk of a lifeguard who *helps* people, a wedding invitation that *invites* people."

Say this twice each day for the next 21 days and it will be tattooed so indelibly in your brain that the steps will pop out in your automatic behaviors when you need them.

Then work on a chapter of this book each week. Read it each day. Concentrate on the action guides. Practice them every chance you get. Evaluate your performance daily. Then go to the next chapter the following week.

This way you'll build powerful habits. You'll take advantage of the learning power of repetition and time lapse.

That's the Customer Satisfaction System. It'll work for you with almost any customer, client, patient, member, guest, patron, or whatever you call your customers.

Use it and you'll be amazed at how quickly people will like you and feel comfortable with you. You'll also be thrilled with how much self-confidence you'll enjoy, as well as how much it will differentiate you from your competitors.

You'll become more valuable to your firm, store, office, or organization. This is just natural, because the more customers like you and return asking for you, the more valuable you'll become. And you'll probably be paid more, as well as feel better about yourself.

You'll help set unseen forces in motion that will increase your own prosperity and success.

HOW TO GET GOOD AT APPLYING THIS SYSTEM

1. Rehearse this memory-stacking system twice each day.
2. Each time associate the exaggerated objects with each of the six steps.
3. Do this for 21 days and then it will be a habit that you do unconsciously.

SOMETHING TO THINK ABOUT

As you practice the Customer-Satisfaction System be sure to accomplish one step before going to the next one—don't skip steps. When all the steps are completed a satisfied customer will result.

DAILY SUCCESS DIARY
Automatically Practicing the Customer-Satisfaction System

This chapter gives you a simple, yet highly effective memory stacking process that will help you have instant recall of the system.

The stacking system will so embed the six steps in your mind that you will practice them automatically. These suggestions will help you turn the ideas into memory.

Please practice the following suggestins and rate your daily performance.

	S	M	T	W	TH	F	S
Customer-Satisfaction System							
1. Repeat the memory-stacking images twice each day.							
2. Identify which step you're doing with each customer.							
3. Don't skip steps.							
Total each day							
Daily average per week							

PART II

SOLVING CUSTOMERS' PROBLEMS

THE PROBLEM-SOLVING FORMULA

1. *Understand* the problem.
2. *Identify* the cause.
3. *Discuss* possible solutions.
4. *Solve* the problem.

Chapter 8

UNDERSTAND THE PROBLEM

"TRY TO UNDERSTAND MY PROBLEM FROM MY VIEWPOINT!"

Everyone has problems. They're simply a way of life. Problems can become stumbling blocks or stepping stones—it all depends on how we deal with them.

Not long ago I was visiting with a senior executive of IBM, and he mentioned that before long they'd manufacture products that required no service—that are problem free.

"You're kidding," I responded. "I didn't know that anything could be made that's problem free.

"Won't producing problem-free products create a lot of other problems?" I asked.

We laughed. Then he answered, "Yeah, well, I suppose it will. It will mean that we don't need several thousand service people we now have."

"Is that a problem?" I asked.

"Yeah," he replied, "We'll have to move many of them to marketing roles."

"Will that create a problem?" I pressed.

"Yeah...the problem is that they don't see themselves in marketing roles."

Inside, I was amused that the elimination of one problem had created several new problems.

Why do I bring this up?

Because problems are a way of life. Everyone has them. And often solving one creates others.

Yes, problems are a way of life. You have them in your work or profession. Everyone else does also. We always will.

YOU GET PAID CONSISTENT WITH YOUR ABILITY TO SOLVE PROBLEMS!

When I was in college a very wise and successful person told me, "Young man, let me tell you something that you'll want to remember...you'll always get paid consistent with your abilities to solve problems."

He went on. "Solve little or no problems and people will want to pay you little or nothing. Solve big problems and people will gladly pay you big dollars!"

I've never forgotten his advice. At the time, I was working afternoons in an office-supply store making 65 cents an hour. So I looked around the store to see what problems I could solve. One that I found was an equipment room full of dust and dirt. So I showed up unannounced in old clothes and cleaned it out. The next week I got a 10-cents-an-hour raise.

In the years since the man told this to me, I've seen his wisdom proven true time and time again. Everytime I've assumed the responsibility of solving new problems I've eventually earned more.

What size problems do you take responsibility for solving, and then solve?

Your pay will usually be consistent.

As a college student I worked as a common laborer during the summers. I didn't get paid much. Today I help large companies increase their sales, customer satisfaction levels, and profitability. I get paid a lot more.

In this book's section you'll learn a simple problem-solving formula. As you learn it and take on the responsibilities of applying the steps, you'll solve more problems. As you solve larger problems, your paycheck will ultimately get larger—either by your present employer or by another one who notices your abilities and wants to increase your pay.

THE PROBLEM-SOLVING FORMULA

In this section you'll learn the following formula:

1. *Understand* the problem.
2. *Identify* the cause.
3. *Discuss* possible solutions.
4. *Solve* the problem.

You'll also learn three action guides for each step. Practicing the action guides will help you do each of the steps well.

This four-step problem-solving formula can be applied in many situations—on the job, with family, or with your own personal problems.

A person from a property-management firm who graduated from our Customer Program writes this about it:

The four-step problem-solving formula will be a lifesaver when handling tenant, owner and maintenance problems.

As a result we are looking for greater productivity, a more pleasant office environment and more satisfied customers.

Here's an excerpt from a doctor, Fred Piper, D.D.S, in Germantown, Tennessee:

Many of the problems we encounter with patients other people experience with customers. The Customer helped all of us develop a systematic way of solving problems that arise with patients. Moreover, our whole approach towards patients and their families has changed...one tangible result is that our referrals from existing patients have increased dramatically.

WHAT A PROBLEM IS

A problem is the difference between what we want to happen and what actually happens.

Please stop and reread this simple definition.

The first step in problem resolution is to understand and identify the problem. Sounds kinda simple, but lots of people who have problems don't know they do.

Like when I bought a winter home in Phoenix and it had to be furnished and carpeted. Within a few days I purchased quite a bit of furniture and carpet. I scheduled it so that the furniture would be delivered on a specific day.

When I paid for the carpet I told the salesperson at Baker Brothers (where I would never buy anything again) that I had to have it installed on a certain day. Then I asked if that was a problem—could he do it?

"No problem," came his response.

"OK," I answered. "Please check on the availability of it and your installer's schedule, because I have to have it on that day."

He checked things out and assured me that it would be installed at 9:00 A.M. on that Thursday.

I called Wednesday afternoon, just to make sure things were OK.

He very casually informed me that it would be another two or three days, maybe a week—he wasn't sure.

"What?" I shot back. "Don't you remember that I told you I had to have it tomorrow when I bought it? And you assured me that it would be done..."

And as nonchalantly as if we were discussing the price of pork in Prussia, he said, "Yeah, well, we had to rearrange things because our larger customers need all our layers then."

"Larger customers," I shrieked, livid at his lack of concern.

"Yeah, well, we have big builders that we sell to."

"Look," I shot back," you took my money with the specific understanding that it would be installed tomorrow morning at 9:00. And I expect it to be done then."

"Well, I don't know," he waffled.

"I will be at my home at 9:00 tomorrow. I will expect your people to be there. I have furniture to be delivered early the following day."

"Well, you call me in the morning and I'll see who we have ahead of you."

"No, I want you to assure me, *right now*, that you'll do what you agreed to do."

"Well, I'll try," came the response, "but if we're not there, you call me."

Sure enough, the next morning they didn't show. At 9:30 I called his store and found out that it was his day off.

I asked to speak to the manager, which took quite a bit of begging; obviously the manager had his calls screened. When I got him, he checked and said that they didn't have me on their schedule and that it would be the middle of next week before they could install it.

I was incensed and told him I would be down there in ten minutes.

He wasn't at all pleased to see me. When I got there I found him to be an egotistical, sold-on-himself person. He wasn't particularly thrilled at my being there, and the feeling was mutual.

It was only after I demanded an immediate refund or his promise to have a crew there by lunch, or I would call the Better Business Bureau, that he assured me that he'd have a crew there by noon.

They finally showed up at 2:00. The crew was friendly and did a good job.

From that moment until now I have never heard from the salesperson or the manager. Neither called or came by to check on the installation.

They could have cared less.

Will I ever go back? Hardly.

Did they have a problem? Was there a difference from my viewpoint between what I wanted to happen and what actually happened?

Did they *understand* their problem?

UNDERSTAND THE PROBLEM

The first step of our Problem Solving Formula is to *understand* the problem. Here are three action guides to practice to help us do this:

1. Get all the facts;
2. Listen nondefensively, and
3. Repeat back the problem as understood.

Effective problem solvers, dealing with small problems or large ones, know first to find out what the problem is, then to set out to solve it. Often, though, they attempt to solve problems before they have all the facts—which is the root of much customer dissatisfaction.

Gordon Payne, service advisor at Phoenix Motor Company, doesn't make that mistake. He patiently listens, getting all the information possible, so he can understand customers' problems.

My car's air conditioner went out during the hottest week in Phoenix history. The temperature hit an all-time high of 122 degrees. Hoping that all it needed was a new fuse, I took my car in, only to find out that it wasn't that simple. After asking me a bunch of questions and checking out several things, Gordon discovered a whole series of problems had occurred. A fan bearing had gone out, causing the car to overheat. This caused something else to blow, which produced more problems. It was like kicking over a bunch of dominoes.

The net result was my air conditioner, radiator, radiator fan, whole fuse assembly—all had to be replaced.

But that wasn't the real problem—at least from my viewpoint. The real problem was that it was just out of warranty by about two months. And, we're talking about a bunch of money.

After taking the time to understand my problem thoroughly he told me that all this didn't just happen at one time, that it probably had begun a few months ago, and that he would go to bat with the manufacturer to see if they would help on the parts.

He could have been talking Greek for all I knew, but I felt that he honestly cared about helping me.

The next day he called me and explained that the manufacturer had agreed to furnish all the parts if I would pay for the labor.

I was thrilled and genuinely grateful for his help.

He followed the action guides of the Problem-Solving Formula. As a result, he cemented his relationship with me and helped me have a very satisfactory service experience.

And...I'll always go back to him.

REMOVE NEGATIVE EMOTIONS FROM PROBLEM SOLVING

One major issue with many problems is the negative or even hostile emotions that occur. Instead of creative problem solving, the relationship often becomes adversarial, with neither side really getting what it wants.

It's easy in the midst of problem resolution for egos to surface and spoil everything. When this happens, good judgment flies out the window. Many customers are lost this way.

At the first knowledge of problems we can react in these ways:

1. Denial or ducking the problem—acting as if it doesn't exist.

2. Blaming or attacking—attempting to push the blame on others.

3. Reacting to customer's anger or negative actions by automatically demonstrating the same behavior.

4. Patiently and calmly getting people talking, venting, and us listening.

When your first objective is to *understand* the problem you'll get all the facts, listen nondefensively, and repeat back the problem as understood.

Asking questions and listening is a terrific strategy to diffuse people's anger or hostility. When you meet their negative tones with calm, sincere understanding, they'll often change, because it takes two to do battle.

Here are some questions that you can ask to help you understand people's problems and defuse their hostile feelings:

1. "So I can understand, would you please explain to me what happened?"
2. "When did you first notice this problem?"
3. "Would you please explain to me everything that has happened?"
4. "Now, to make sure I understand, would you please explain all this one more time?"

Often, if you can get people to explain their view of the problem twice they'll talk out their negative feelings or anger. Then if you'll listen nondefensively, without interrupting or arguing, their negative emotions will evaporate.

DON'T ARGUE ABOUT WHO CREATED THE PROBLEM

The Ritz-Carlton Hotels have a policy that when any employee spots a problem he or she is to "take ownership" of it. It becomes the employee's problem to handle as best as he or she can.

"Taking ownership" of a problem is saying, "Hey, we have a problem, and it's my responsibility to solve it."

It wasn't this way when I bought a pair of slacks in Saks Fifth Avenue. The salesperson fitted them, marking where to hem the legs. When I went back to pick them up I tried them on to double-check them. The hem was up two to three inches from where it should have been. You could see my ankles and socks. It reminded me of when I was a teenager in the '50s and we rolled our jeans' legs up almost to the tops of our white socks.

"This will never do," I told the salesperson. "I can't wear them like this. You'll have to let them out."

He looked at them and said, "We can't let them out, there's not enough fabric left."

Well, there was plenty when I first tried them on, and the mistake was definitely their fault, so I responded, "Someone obviously made a mistake. All I want is for them to look right."

"We would never have marked the hem here unless you had told us to," he shot back, becoming very defensive and obviously blaming me for the problem.

He then proceeded to make a federal case out of the whole deal. I finally told him that all I wanted was a pair that had the hem at the right place. Very reluctantly, he agreed to alter another pair for me.

I couldn't believe it. He was attempting to blame me for the problem. Who in his right mind would ever think that I wanted the pants cut off halfway to my knees?

I've never been back to buy anything. I've almost gone in several times, but my memory of that experience keeps me away.

The funny part is that he could have used that experience to cement a relationship with me. He could have admitted that they messed up, while assuring me that it would be quickly corrected. We could both have laughed and gone on.

Really, it was no big deal. The weight of the world didn't exactly rest on my having the slacks in the first place.

It was so ridiculous for him to try to pin the blame on me. If he had simply taken ownership of the problem—admitted it and assured me that he'd correct it, I would have been happy. And...they would have made more money from my future purchases.

IN SUMMARY

Everyone has problems. They just happen. They always will.

Problems can have positive or negative consequences. They can cause customers to become unhappy and leave your firm, or they can build stronger relationships with them.

It all has to do with how you respond and react to them.

In this chapter you learned the first step of our Problem-Solving Formula. You learned to first understand the problem.

As you go about understanding problems, get all the facts, listen nondefensively, and then repeat back the problem as you understand it. When you have a sincere desire to understand problems, you'll defuse the anger, hostility, or negative feelings that customers have.

In order to do this, though, you'll have to keep a careful check on your own ego and emotions. To become defensive, to deny responsibility, or to blame customers will almost always create more problems than it solves.

This and the following chapters can help you become a better problem solver. When you practice the action guides you'll have more confidence in the face of problems and you'll discover a way to deepen your relationships with customers.

And the payoff is that you'll usually earn more or in some way be compensated to a greater degree, because you'll be paid consistent with your abilities to solve problems.

HOW TO GET GOOD AT
***UNDERSTANDING* PROBLEMS**

1. Get all the facts.
2. Listen nondefensively.
3. Repeat back the problem as understood.

SOMETHING TO THINK ABOUT

"Taking ownership" or responsibility for problems, when done with a sincere desire to understand them and solve them, can turn negative customer attitudes into positive ones.

RULES FOR ALIENATING CUSTOMERS

Should you discover your business prospering too much, or your prosperity making too many demands on you, here are some rules that will surely return you to your desired level of poverty.

Should you be cynical and doubt that they'll work for you, be assured that millions of other people have proven these rules to be very effective in keeping them at their desired low levels of success.

1. Deny any responsibility for problems that come up.
2. Place the blame on customers where, of course, it belongs.
3. When it's not in your department, shove it off on other people.
4. Tell customers where they can go to get their problems solved instead of taking them.
5. Carefully manage your priorities so you won't have to waste time on customer problems.
6. Change jobs to other places where customers don't hassle you so much with their problems.

Yeah, these are popular strategies for people who want to insure that they aren't faced with the inevitable problems that result from success and prosperity.

DAILY SUCCESS DIARY
UNDERSTAND THE PROBLEM

You face problems each day. Customers may be calm or irate, but they have problems they want you to solve.

This week, read this chapter and focus on understanding the problems people have. Practice the action guides and rate your performance daily.

	S	M	T	W	TH	F	S
Understand the Problem							
1. Get all the facts.							
2. Listen nondefensively.							
3. Repeat back the problems as understood.							
Total each day							
Daily average per week							

Chapter 9

IDENTIFY THE CAUSE OF THE PROBLEM

"TAKE ENOUGH TIME TO UNDERSTAND WHAT CAUSED MY PROBLEM!"

Every problem has a cause. Something happened that caused every problem to occur. Effective problem solving happens when the cause is identified and removed or remedied.

This principle holds true for the customer-service problems you have. Identify and remove the cause and the problem will often be solved.

Remembering this principle will help you work toward solving the problems you encounter.

You have learned that the first step in problem solving is understanding the problem. In this chapter we'll learn about the second step—identifying the cause.

IDENTIFYING THE CAUSE OF PROBLEMS

To solve a problem you have to identify the cause—the *real* cause—then remove or remedy it.

There are many causes of problems. They can be functional—the fuel line in my car's engine clogged up. They can be personal—a salesperson's attitude or the manner in which I was treated. Some problems are preventable and some aren't.

In order to identify the real cause you can ask these questions:

1. "What has happened?"
2. "What should have happened?"
3. "What went wrong?"

Asking and answering these questions can help you get at the root of a problem. When you ask these questions in a sincere, nonaggressive way you'll impress people with your professionalism.

I'll never forget an experience I had years ago when I owned a retail furniture business. One of my best customers, who had purchased a considerable amount of furniture for her home and office, called me one day, very upset.

Without taking time to even say "Hello," she stormed, "What are you trying to do to us?"

Before I could even think or respond, she went on, "What makes you think you can cheat us on this statement and get by with it?"

Again, before I could get a word in edgeways, she screamed, "With all the money we've spent with you—and now you try to get to us—I thought we could trust you..."

She raged on and on, peppering her accusations with some very colorful language.

After a few moments, which seemed like an eternity, she slowed down. Finally, I asked her what the problem was. "You overcharged me on this mattress...and I don't like it...." She stormed into a rage again, repeating everything she had previously said to me, louder this time.

"What do you mean?" I finally had a chance to ask back.

"You charged me too much!" she responded.

"Let me pull a copy of the invoice," I said.

When I got it I told her that the price was correct. She then got more intense. "You're lying to me," she shouted. "How do I know but what you've overcharged me on everything you sold me? If you've cheated me this time, you've probably done it other times!"

For the life of me I couldn't figure out what she was talking about, so I told her that I'd be right out and talk to her.

The price I had given her was correct. And besides, she never really cared what the price was anyway. She bought the best and never even asked what the price was. None of it made sense.

When I got to her home I showed her the invoice and the catalog price. To this she snorted and took me into the bedroom, ripped the covers off the foot of the mattress and pointed at the label.

In those days all major brand mattresses had large labels pressed in them with the name and suggested retail price. Immediately, I knew the source of her anger. The factory had put the wrong label on the mattress, and we hadn't caught it. Hers was a Sealy Posturpedic, which was the most expensive, but which had a less expensive label on it.

I explained this to her. She didn't want to believe me; I suppose because then she wouldn't have any reason to vent her anger. I offered to bring out a new one that had the proper tag on it. I even offered to call the factory and let her talk to the sales manager who would verify the price I had charged her.

It was only when I invited her to the store to see mattresses like hers, and to see the price tag on them, and then look at ones that had labels like the one that was mistakenly put on hers, that she began to believe me.

So, what was the problem...and what was the cause?

The problem was that she felt cheated and taken advantage of. The cause was the misapplied label. A deeper cause could have been her own self-esteem. She was a very abrasive, easy-to-set-off person.

It was only by asking, "What has happened? What should have happened? What went wrong?" that I was able to eventually solve the problem.

Egos, EMOTIONS, ATTITUDES

Problems or complaints aren't usually logical, nor can they be solved by mere logic. When people's emotions enter the picture, logic often goes out the window. This makes problem solving difficult and is why we occasionally fail to solve problems or complaints.

In complaining, people often place themselves in a position where their egos won't allow them to retreat or accept solutions. This is why we should do everything possible to neutralize negative emotions.

One effective way to neutralize these harmful emotions is to admit your fault quickly. To say with your words and actions, "Hey, it's my responsibility—the cause of the problem can rest on my shoulders. I'll take full blame. My main objective is to correct the problem and make you happy."

When that's your attitude, you'll undoubtedly neutralize the hostile and enraged emotions that your customers can have.

Rather than putting the responsibility of the problem or its cause and cure on your customer's shoulders, place it on your own.

Don't allow yourself to become trapped into discussing where the blame should rest. You can't win that game. Keep egos out of the way.

How MUCH DOES AN UNRESOLVED COMPLAINT COST YOU?

Few people have any idea how much an unresolved complaint costs them.

An auto-parts company owner brought this question to my attention. He said, "Whenever customers have a problem or are unhappy, I ask them what they feel needs to be done to correct it and whatever they say, I do."

"Really?" I asked. "Anything?"

"Yeah," he responded. "Look at it like this. If I have to give a part away, I still come out ahead—even if I'm right and they're dead wrong."

He went on, "If I have to charge off a $50 part, it's still a lot less than losing the several thousand dollars that their future business would have brought in.

"The real issue," he explained, "isn't what their complaint is. The real issue is what I'll lose in future business if they decide to take their business elsewhere."

He knew the reality of what an unresolved complaint could cost him.

How much does an unresolved complaint cost you?

I asked myself this question recently as I left a dry cleaners. Because of its convenient location, I had selected this new one. On my first visit I paid them $32 for shirts and cleaning. On the next trip my bill was $26, plus a pair of slacks to be taken up in the waist.

When I paid I noticed that the charge for the pants was $19. This seemed expensive, because I'd just had several pairs altered at an upscale men's shop and they cost only $10 each.

"Nineteen dollars!" I said. "Why so much?"

The person didn't know why, and was clearly ticked off that I had questioned him. "Look, all I wanted was for you to take them up in the waist and taper them down to the crotch," I explained. "Your sign says $9.50. Why are you charging me $19?" He didn't know.

"Where's your manager?" I asked.

He went and got the manager—a rather rotund person who looked as if he'd hate anyone automatically who had to have his pants taken up.

He wasn't too thrilled at my question either.

"What's the problem?" he grunted.

"Why am I being charged $19 when your sign there says $9.50?"

Without blinking he replied, "Yeah, I remember them, we had to do two different alterations on 'em."

"Two?" I asked.

"We had to alter the crotch also."

"I feel like I've been taken advantage of," I said. "Why didn't you tell me how much they were going to be when I brought them in?"

He went into a lengthy explanation that I neither understood nor had the patience to endure. So I paid him and left. He had won. He got what he wanted. I suppose he was happy that he had made an extra $9.50. But his victory boxed me in to the point that my ego would never allow me to go back, even though I wanted to continue stopping there because of its convenience.

How did he actually fare in that transaction? Well, look at it like this: he made $9.50 and lost $3,000!

Three thousand dollars? Yeah, that's about what I would have spent with him in the next three or four years if he had satisfied me. Just think, even if I had been dead wrong, had he apologized and offered to adjust the price he could have cemented my business and developed a trust relationship with me. I would have appreciated his concern and felt in his debt.

What does an unresolved complaint cost you or your firm? And how much can you add to your company's profitability by speedily resolving the ones that happen?

It's important to understand how much an unresolved complaint costs you. Here are some of the factors to consider when you assess your real costs:

1. What the issue at hand costs to satisfy.
2. What the future purchases of this customer will be.
3. What future business will be influenced by this customer — if he or she is happy or unhappy.

In a study that was conducted by the Washington, D.C.-based Technical Assistance Research Programs, Inc., the following conclusions were reached:

1. For every customer who bothers to complain to the average business, there are 26 others who remain silent.
2. The average "wronged" customer will tell 8 to 16 people. (More than 10 percent will tell more than 20 people.)
3. Ninety-one percent of unhappy customers will never purchase goods or services from you again.
4. If you make an effort to remedy customers' complaints, 82 to 95 percent will stay with you.
5. It costs about five times as much to attract a new customer as it costs to keep an old one.

The statistics from this prominent research firm speak for themselves.

As you look at them, how do you relate them to your business or profession?

It's important that you ask and answer this question.

IDENTIFYING THE PROBLEM'S CAUSE HELPS TO AVOID COMBAT

Whatever you do—whether you're a medical technician, an attorney, a dental assistant, or a retail clerk—you can defuse negative emotions by proving your sincere desire to understand the cause of a problem so you can solve it.

It's at this point that your objectivity and professionalism will impress people. When you say with your attitude and actions, "I want to understand the problem and its cause so I can effectively reach a solution and satisfy you!" people will be positively impressed.

When you objectively ask,

"What has happened?"
"What should have happened?"
"What went wrong?"

And when you listen without biases, your actions will have a strong psychological impact on people.

This sincere listening strategy will powerfully defuse people's anger and hostility. It's a potent psychological strategy.

LISTENING NONDEFENSIVELY

As you attempt to understand the cause of a problem, it helps to listen nondefensively. Listen without preconceived notions or biases.

Now, I'll have to admit that this isn't exactly easy to do, but you can make it a habit by practicing it.

Leni Patton, gift-shop manager aboard the SS *Norway*, wrote about how she benefited from listening nondefensively to customers.

> Learning the problem-solving formula helped me the most. When I applied it, passengers seemed happier with the outcomes.
>
> I've learned to let them talk (no matter how long) and I'm more aware of listening nondefensively. I realized the passengers were ready for me to be defensive and when I didn't act that way, solving their problems became so painless for both of us.
>
> Before your program, when a dissatisfied passenger came to me, my attitude was, "Here we go again." Now problems are easier because I know they will be solved positively. I now have the awareness and control to change situations into the right perspective.

One of her associates on the cruise line wrote this about her new ability to solve problems:

> The most important benefit I have learned from the program is problem solving. To take the time to listen and understand all angles of a problem.

When it is understood, then it becomes less of a problem and works out well for all parties involved.

Without the ability to listen patiently and with an open mind the problems will only increase and cause unsatisfied service.

What's the cause of most of your problems?

Take a moment and think of the most common problems you experience with customers. Most problems can fall into these four main categories:

1. Functional—The product or service didn't work right.
2. Misapplication—People didn't put it together or use it correctly.
3. Human element—Imperfect people don't make things that are perfect nor do imperfect people perfectly use or maintain them.
4. Ego—How this problem causes people to look good or bad in the eyes of themselves and others.

Look at these four categories again and see if number 4 doesn't account for about 80 percent of your problems? Can't the cause of most misunderstandings be traced back to ego reasons?

How easy is it for you to allow your ego to become involved in your problem resolution? Let's be honest, it's easy, isn't it?

IN SUMMARY

Remember that every problem has a cause. It may be readily apparent, or it may take some digging to uncover it.

Generally, when you discover and remove the cause you'll solve the problem.

Now, it may be easy to identify the cause of your customer's problems. Someone may just want to exchange a suit or return a sweater. Or it can be more complex. Maybe someone's television cable is on the blink, and you have to trace down the cause of the problem. Perhaps you work in a medical lab, and you have to discover the reason why a patient is ill.

Your problems may have to do with direct customers, clients, patients, or guests, or with internal customers—people in your organization whom you support.

When confronted with a problem, your sincere attitude of, "Hey, I want to understand the cause of the problem so I can satisfy you," will impress people.

Remember especially to keep your ego out of the way. Deny yourself the pleasure of pinning the blame on someone else. Instead, assume responsibility of owning the problem and satisfying people. Or, as the Ritz Carlton Hotel chain tells their people—"Take ownership of the problem." Take responsibility for doing everything you can to solve it.

Learn and practice using the Problem-Solving Formula and you'll develop more confidence in dealing with negative issues. And, the more effective you are in solving problems, the higher you'll go in your organization.

HOW TO GET GOOD AT IDENTIFYING THE CAUSES OF PROBLEMS

1. Find out what has happened.
2. Find out what should have happened.
3. Find out what went wrong.

SOMETHING TO THINK ABOUT

A problem whose cause is understood is half solved!

STRATEGIES FOR BEATING CUSTOMERS AT THEIR OWN GAME

The following strategies will enable and empower you to keep the upper hand and beat customers before they beat you.

These steps will also help you keep your own ego intact and ultimately win over people.

1. Before hearing customers, first explain company policy and guidelines for handling problems or complaints.
2. Always remember that all buyers are liars!
3. Whenever customers are obviously wrong, you should be honest and tell them so.
4. Quickly brand certain customers as chronic complainers and tune them out.
5. Stoutly defend your position when you're right and customers are wrong.
6. Never give refunds or exchanges to customers who you're sure only want to take advantage of you.

Yeah, hey, just try these strategies and you'll effectively show customers who's in control. Of course, you may work yourself out of a job pretty soon. But in that event, you can always get into politics or government work, where you'll find the above strategies very helpful.

DAILY SUCCESS DIARY
IDENTIFY THE CAUSE

In this chapter you learned that every problem has a cause and that once you understand a problem and its cause, you're well on your way to solving it.

As you focus on this step this week, record your daily successes.

	S	M	T	W	TH	F	S
Identify the Cause							
1. Find out what happened.							
2. Find out what should have happened.							
3. Find out what went wrong.							
Total each day							
Daily average per week							

Chapter 10

DISCUSS **POSSIBLE SOLUTIONS**

"EXPLORE POSSIBLE SOLUTIONS WITH ME!"

Someone once remarked that customers will help us solve most of our problems with them if we'll only let them. One way you can move toward problem resolution, as well as show your concern and sensitivity to people, is to discuss possible solutions with them.

Not only does this create an air of professionalism, it also helps you move beyond arguments, conflicts, or discussions about who should shoulder the blame.

You'll resolve conflicts much faster and keep your customers happy when you seek out options and then help them select the best ones.

This works from the most simple situations to the most complicated ones. Let me share a couple of stories that prove this.

The first one happened just last week. I was in a doctor's reception room to get the results of a physical exam I had taken a few days earlier.

An elderly couple came in and told the receptionist that they had an appointment and gave her their name. She looked at her schedule book and informed them that their appointment was at 11:00 and it was now 10:00. Confused, they looked at each other and the man said to the woman (men always blame women for their problems), "But you told me it was at 10:00 o'clock!"

To which she replied, "I did not, I told you I didn't remember. You said it was at 10:00!"

He wasn't too thrilled at that and grumbled his displeasure, which precipitated a couple of minutes of rather active dialogue between them.

All the time the receptionist just sat there and didn't say a word—which was probably smart—as the old saying goes, "Discretion is the better part of valor!"

Sizing up her problem, the woman asked the receptionist, "Well, what are we gonna do? It's too far back home and we don't have time to go to Walmart and do the rest of our shopping!"

The receptionist just looked at the couple and didn't say a word.

They waited for her to suggest the possible solutions and help solve their problem. She obviously didn't get the message.

Again, one asked the other, "What'll we do for the next hour?"

Neither knew. Both seemed very confused. Again the receptionist didn't help. She didn't offer any options or say anything. In fact, she was hoping to get them out of her hair so she could go back to her posting, or whatever she was doing.

After a painful moment of indecision, the man asked her if they could just sit in the reception room and look at magazines for the next hour.

The receptionist replied dryly, "Yes," and they sat down.

I asked myself, Why wasn't she more sensitive? Common sense would tell you to at least say something. Did this medical receptionist realize that she could have helped them solve a problem? One that wasn't any big deal to her, but was to them?

Obviously, she didn't.

A PROBLEM MAY BE LARGE OR SMALL, BUT IT'S STILL A PROBLEM!

Now, you may think my story of the couple in the doctor's office is a small, insignificant problem. In a way it was; in a way it wasn't. It was important to those elderly people at the time it happened.

But see how easily the Problem-Solving Formula could have been applied. See how it would have taken only a minute for the receptionist to:

1. *Understand* the problem.
2. *Identify* the cause.
3. *Discuss* possible solutions.
4. *Solve* the problem.

Had she done this, the couple would have experienced much less tension and confusion, and she would have shown her concern for them—all making her, and the couple, feel much better.

A couple of years ago I designed a Trade Assistance program for Chevrolet branches to use to settle disputes with unhappy customers. Traditionally, when a customer couldn't get a problem resolved with a dealer and called a Chevrolet branch, the customer would be referred to a Better Business Bureau for arbitration.

This process made about as much sense as two people who had a disagreement going out into the back alley and slugging it out so they could become friends. When put into this adversarial role, disgruntled customers came away hating both Chevrolet and the dealer.

And since Chevrolet wanted to keep the customer for life, they thought there must be a better way to settle disputes and keep customers' loyalty.

In the course of working with them I heard a story about a man we'll call "The General."

The General was a retired, high-ranking military officer who owned a Chevy truck. After experiencing several problems, and not getting satisfaction from the dealer, he began to flood huge numbers of people at Chevrolet with letters. He rattled sabres from the top to the bottom of the organization—threatening lawsuits and anything else he could think of. He quickly gained fame among Chevrolet people—like a skunk in a perfume shop.

Finally, a branch employee called and talked to him in a very mild tone that got through the General's abrasiveness and anger. The employee listened quietly while the old soldier expressed his feelings for the dozenth time.

Apparently, no one had ever really listened to the General; everyone had responded aggressively, which of course didn't work at all. But this time he vented his wrath while a wise person listened patiently.

Finally, after he had expelled much of his feelings the branch person explained that one option would be to trade in his truck for a new one, with special credit being given him.

"Oh, NO!" the General responded. That wasn't what he wanted at all. He loved the truck, and despite the problem, wanted to keep it.

As it turned out, all he wanted someone to do was listen to him, take him seriously, and offer him some options.

He didn't want to exercise any of the options, because that wasn't the real issue.

The real issue was that he wanted to be heard and listened to.

The General loved the nice branch person and began to write letters to people in Chevrolet praising him.

Interesting lesson, isn't it?

ACTION GUIDES TO PRACTICE

For almost any problem, you can discuss possible solutions by practicing these action guides:

1. Suggest options.
2. Ask for customers' ideas.
3. Agree on the best course of action.

When you methodically apply these steps you'll usually get very positive results.

SUGGEST OPTIONS

Chevrolet people learned that by giving customers more options they made happier customers. In this case the extra option was to trade the old car in for a new one and receive a more than fair price for the old vehicle. This showed Chevrolet's care, concern, and sensitivity to the customer's problem.

It also allowed the customer to focus on the option, rather than on the conflict.

When you have a problem with a customer, what different options do you have? What different solutions or alternatives can you offer to make the customer happy?

The medical receptionist mentioned earlier in this chapter could have offered the following solutions when the elderly couple's problem was identified.

1. She could have invited them to sit down and read magazines while she got them a cup of coffee.
2. She might have verbalized her concern for their situation, told them of a coffee shop three blocks away, and given them three dollars to pay for their coffee.
3. She could have suggested they stroll through the outdoor Arizona Center, which was only five minutes away.

But she didn't, so she blew a great opportunity to go the extra mile and cement her relationship with the couple. Doing this would not only have made the doctor more money in the long haul, it would have impressed those of us in the waiting room.

But hey, who knows, conditions may get so competitive that even doctors, their nurses and receptionists start being nice to patients!

Ask for customers' ideas

I had ordered a pair of casual pants from the L. L. Bean catalogue. When they arrived, the length was not what I had ordered. They were too long.

Now it would have been easy to send them back. In fact that's exactly what I intended to do—for months. The "I'll do it tomorrow, I'm too busy to do it today" syndrome lasted for more than six months. Meanwhile I had thrown the sales slip away.

Finally, embarrassed at my procrastination, I decided to seize the moment and take bold action. So I called the toll-free number and told the nice telephone person my problem, half expecting her to deny any liability because of my laziness and neglect.

To my surprise she informed me very cheerfully that I could still send them back. She told me how to mark them.

So I sent them back. But I didn't get the new pair. In about a month I called and got an equally nice person. I told her what had happened, fully expecting her to deny any liability and tell me that unless I could produce evidence that I had sent them back, that she wouldn't send another pair.

But she didn't. She apparently pulled my record up on her computer screen and, without questioning my actions, apologized and offered these options.

1. To send a new pair of slacks to me immediately.
2. Credit my American Express account for the original amount, plus the postage I was out in sending them back.
3. Give me credit toward another purchase.

Not once did she question my integrity or word. She was friendly and extremely helpful. The result was that I ordered a couple of sweaters from her as well as the pants.

But the real result was the good taste she left in my mouth for L. L. Bean—which, of course, meant that they would get a lot more of my dollars in the future.

By explaining the options and asking for my ideas, she allowed me to help solve my own problem. By drawing me into the decision, she got me talking, which gave her a chance to listen to me. Her listening gave her a chance to gain rapport with me, which gave her a chance to cement a relationship with me.

I felt great about doing business with them.

I don't feel so wonderful about doing business with a certain bank here in Arizona who will go unnamed.

When interest rates dropped several points I decided to refinance my house. I had an adjustable mortgage, and it had gone up to where it was 3½ points above what current interest rates were on 15-year fixed-rate mortgages.

I applied at the bank and was told that a deposit of $350 was required, but that it would be returned to me if they didn't make the loan. So I gave them my deposit and they locked in a rate that was good for 45 days.

They gave me a list of all the papers they'd need, and I got all the forms filled out and everything in to them. Some guy came out and did an appraisal. I waited to hear from them. A month went by, no contract. I called them, only to be talked down to by a snippy young woman in some scary sounding department.

Finally, she said I'd have to fill in more forms and send her more information. So I did. Nothing happened. I called back. Got the same person. She made me feel like a criminal that couldn't be trusted. I filled in more forms.

Nothing happened.

Four months later I called again and asked what was taking so long. She wanted me to sign an affidavit about income. I didn't see any sense in this, since I had given them my last three years' income tax forms.

Finally her yawniness and could-care-less attitude prevailed, and I asked her to bundle up everything and send it back to me, along with the $350 check.

She informed me that they wouldn't send the check back. I asked her why and she said, "We don't send the deposit checks back if you decide not to get a loan from us."

"But all the loan officers I talked to said that if you didn't make the loan that I'd get my money back. You haven't made the loan, so I want my money back."

She stoutly repeated that I wouldn't get it. I told her what I thought of her customer service. She clearly didn't care how I felt. I'll assure you that the New England Patriots will win the Super Bowl before I ever go in that bank again.

Despite her inefficiency and total no-care attitude I would have forgiven the bank if she had apologized and sent my deposit back. The $350 was nothing; it was the principle of it all.

Agree on the Best Course of Action

If the bank person had asked me what I felt was the best way to solve our problem, I would have been forgiving. But she didn't, and the last thing I'll ever do is go back.

Psychologically speaking, when we ask for customers' ideas about the best course of action, we usually cause them to become more lenient and forgiving. We cause them to soften from the often firm positions they feel forced to defend. It makes it all right for them to compromise.

The question, "What do you feel is the best solution?" often causes disgruntled people to become much more pliable and easy to work with.

IN SUMMARY

In this chapter we have thought about the third step of our Problem-Solving Formula—*Discuss* possible solutions.

I suggested that you look for alternatives, options, and possible solutions and discuss these with customers. We learned to ask for customers' ideas and then really to listen to them.

I mentioned that the Formula can be used for small problems or large ones. I challenged you to think of yourself as a problem solver—regardless of what kind of work or profession you're in.

As you reflect on the ideas in this chapter, I'd like to leave you with a definite action step. Practicing it will help you solve problems naturally. Take a moment and write your answers to the following questions.

Hey, don't get lazy on me. C'mon, get up and grab a pen and write your answers to these questions.

1. What is one common problem your customers have?

_____

_____

_____

_____

_____

_____

_____

_____

2. What are some possible solutions to this problem?

a. _____

_____

_____

_____

b. _____

_____

_____

_____

c. _____

_____

_____

_____

d. _____

_____

_____

_____

Now, take a moment and analyze what you've done. You have identified a problem and some possible solutions. In doing this you have simply done a logical process.

Translate this to your work. Get in the habit of mentally defining a problem you have and automatically thinking of possible solutions. When you do this and mention them to your customers, as you ask for their ideas and responses, you'll become much more skilled at solving problems.

And the better you get at solving problems the more someone will be willing to pay you.

**HOW TO GET GOOD AT DISCUSSING
POSSIBLE SOLUTIONS**

1. Suggest options.
2. Ask for customers' ideas.
3. Agree on best course of action.

SOMETHING TO THINK ABOUT

Not only will you enhance problem resolution, but valuing customers' ideas and listening intently to them will help fill emotional and ego needs they have.

SUGGESTIONS FOR DODGING PROBLEMS EFFECTIVELY

Here are some suggestions that will help you achieve two objectives. First, you'll waste little time with negative people who want to bore you with their problems, and second, you'll be able to get back to more frequent coffee breaks, visiting with friends over the telephone, and discussing your crummy management with other employees.

1. Know ahead of time exactly how you'll handle customer complaints or problems. This will save you a lot of time listening, which will free up a lot of time for more creative activities.
2. Enforce a strict policy that allows no exceptions.
3. Don't get emotionally involved with customers; it'll only create more stress for you.
4. Remember, people will always take advantage of you if you let them, so be smart and don't let that happen.

DAILY SUCCESS DIARY
DISCUSS POSSIBLE SOLUTIONS

The next step in solving problems, once they've been understood and their causes identified, is to look at options—discuss possible solutions.

When you take time to do this with customers you'll show your interest and sincere desire to help them. You'll also be much more effective in helping people.

	S	M	T	W	TH	F	S
Discuss Possible Solutions							
1. Suggest options.							
2. Ask for customers' ideas.							
3. Agree on the best course of action.							
Total each day							
Daily average per week							

Chapter 11

SOLVE
THE PROBLEM

"SOLVE MY PROBLEMS AND YOU'LL ENJOY MY LOYALTY FOREVER!"

As you do the first three steps of the Problem-Solving Formula, you'll often find that the problem soon gets solved.

Said another way, problems are close to being resolved when you:

1. *Understand* the problem.
2. *Identify* the cause.
3. *Discuss* possible solutions.

When these steps are successfully accomplished and you follow the action guides for the fourth step, you'll enjoy problem resolution as well as the respect and appreciation of satisfied customers.

ACTION GUIDES FOR SOLVING THE PROBLEM

The three action guides that will help you solve problems, once the first three steps have been done, are:

1. Remove the cause, or
2. Take corrective action.
3. Ask if the customer is satisfied with resolution.

REMOVE THE CAUSE

As I've written before—every problem has a cause, and when the cause is removed or corrective action taken, it usually gets solved.

Once it's identified, a problem's cause is often easy to remove. Other times it isn't.

Like when Mr. Aronson, a retired accountant, went into the city water department, upset at the amount of his water bill.

Normally a soft spoken, logical person, he threw his monthly bill down on the counter, jutted his jaw, and barked at the cashier, "This is an outrage! Why do you think I could have used this much water? You expect me to pay for your mistake? Why is this month's bill three times what it should be? Someone made a mistake! What do I pay taxes for? To get treated like this?"

Mr. Aronson spent the next few minutes expelling his emotions about the overcharging. The cashier quietly listened, showing no defensiveness.

Finally, when Mr. Aronson had vented his anger and was feeling a bit guilty for it, the cashier smiled at him and said, "I'm very sorry for this problem, Mr. Aronson. This does look excessive."

"Excessive?" he replied. "I should be so rich as to pay for it! What do you think, that I'm the First National or something?"

She smiled, "Well, let me apologize. And, let me assure you that if this is a mistake we'll find the reason and correct it."

"I should think so," he replied.

"You say that this is three times as much as your water charges normally are?"

He nodded affirmatively.

She punched in her computer, and his monthly charges came up on the screen. She viewed them.

"Well," she smiled at him, "you are correct, Mr. Aronson. It does seem that this is over three times what your monthly charges are."

"So...tell me something I don't know," he replied.

She went on, "There are several reasons why this could have happened."

"Look, I'm retired. Rockefeller, I'm not. I refuse to pay this amount!"

"I can understand how you feel, Mr. Aronson. And we certainly don't want you to pay for something that's more than you owe.

"As I said, there are several possible causes. Before you pay anything let me have someone look into it. I'll introduce you to my supervisor, Ms. Nash. She's very good at solving customers' problems."

Ms. Nash outlined four possible causes of the problem: (1) their computers malfunctioned; (2) the meter was read inaccurately; (3) the meter was malfunctioning; or (4) there was a leak in the water line. She assured Mr. Aronson that she'd send a service person out to inspect the meter and make sure it was measuring accurately.

The service person found that the meter was accurately measuring the water going through, so that wasn't the cause. It also showed the same amount of water as the monthly statement. He explained to Mr. Aronson that the meter was accurate, and that he had, indeed, used the quantity of water that he had been charged for.

Mr. Aronson wasn't too thrilled to hear this and vigorously expressed his feelings, as well as his view of the city's accuracy.

The service person explained that since the meter was accurate, there was no point in checking the computer's billing. Mr. Aronson didn't feel wonderful about this, either.

After a careful inspection of his plumbing was undertaken, the cause was identified. Mr. Aronson had a small guest room attached to his home. It had one bedroom and a bath. Since he and his wife had had no guests for several months, the room was closed. They had simply not looked in it.

The city supervisor found that the float valve on the toilet had corroded, causing a constant stream of water down the drain. This leakage could normally be heard as a strange sound in the water pipes, but both the Aronsons had experienced hearing loss and didn't hear the sound.

The customer-service person carefully explained the problem and cut the water off to that toilet until they could get a repair person out.

The cause was identified and corrected, and the problem was solved.

Now, not all problems are this clear and easy to resolve—some are, some aren't. But the principle is the same: find the cause and correct it and the problem usually gets corrected.

Take corrective action

Mr. Aronson's problem was solved when the customer-service clerk took corrective action. Mr. Aronson wasn't overly eager to pay the water bill. But it was clearly his responsibility. He admitted and understood that.

The result was that he felt the city had served him well. He appreciated the courtesy, concern, and professionalism of the cashier, the supervisor, and the customer-service person.

Now, you probably don't work for the city, but you have your own special problems to solve. Your professionalism shows when you have a good grasp of the common problems your customers have and when you know what corrective action to take once the cause of a problem has been identified.

It's here that your sincere desire to help customers can be further shown. Your attitude is demonstrated in your actions.

When people see that you want to help them, your trust and rapport will be increased. This gives you a terrific opportunity to cement relationships with customers that will cause them to want to continue to do business with you.

It's the manner and attitude with which you take corrective action that influences much of your customers' satisfaction.

I've often experienced problems where corrective action was taken, but it was done in a grudging, suspicious, surly way.

I have a friend who purchased a dress at a nice shop. When she got home she found a flaw in the weave of the cloth. It was a week before she took it back. When she did the clerk who sold it to her wasn't in, so another one looked at the dress critically and responded, "Yes, we'll allow you to return it, but are you sure you haven't worn it?"

My friend was incensed at the rudeness and suspicion of the clerk.

It's all in our attitudes. Along this line I often remember the reputed example of customer service that Rolls-Royce offered. It seemed that a wealthy Arab experienced problems with his Rolls' transmission. A telegram was sent to the dealer in London who had sold and shipped the vehicle.

With no fanfare a service person was flown to the location of the automobile and a new transmission was installed. He then flew back to London.

The owner received no billing for the service and telegrammed the dealer to ask why he had received no bill. Immediately, he received a telegram that said:

> Thank you for your wire. Stop. We are sorry but we have no record of a Rolls-Royce transmission ever failing. Stop. But if it ever occurs we will replace it at no charge. Stop.

Now that was customer service.

ASK IF CUSTOMER IS SATISFIED WITH RESOLUTION

Here's one you won't believe.

I had contacted some kind of stomach bug. It hung around for over a month. Finally, after all the self-administered remedies failed to work, I figured it wasn't going away. So I went to a new doctor, who was very nice and thorough in explaining everything to me. After several tests he gave me some pills to take, which did clear up the bug.

I was impressed at his kindness and diligence in explaining everything to me in an unhurried way. In fact, I was so accustomed to doctors backing out of the room when I asked them questions that I felt guilty about this one being nice and helpful.

Three or four days later he called me at my office to see how I was feeling. I couldn't believe it—a doctor calling to see how I felt. What a shocker!

I recently had extensive dental work done. It included removal of all mercury fillings, the installation of new porcelain crowns and porcelain laminates.

The work was done by Dr. Bill Gregg in El Toro, California. After my three lengthy visits to his office I received a letter thanking me, along with two calls from Dr. Gregg and Sharon, one of his staff people.

It was obvious that they cared about me and wanted to know if their work was satisfactory.

How to cement strong customer relationships

There's a special point where your sincere concern and interest in customers pays big dividends for you. It's when the sale has been made, the work has been done, the patient released—after you've done whatever you do with customers, clients, patients, members, or guests, and you contact them to see how they're doing.

When you follow up with customers to see how your problem resolution is working and lay yourself open to potential happiness or unhappiness—it's here that you make the most points with people.

Your genuine, sincere desire to know how they're doing will positively impact people with maximum results.

The reason is simple: Few people actually take the time to say, "Thank you," or, "How are you doing, feeling, or liking what you bought?" or, "What is your level of satisfaction?"

Few people take the time to show their concern and appreciation and do follow-ups.

When you do, you'll make lasting impressions on your customers.

IT'S ACTUALLY ONLY COMMON COURTESY

What I'm suggesting is actually only common courtesy. But come to think about it, it isn't all that common!

Think I'm being too harsh or critical? Hey, all you have to do is observe the people you do business with to see that common courtesy isn't all that common.

"The flight has been delayed," the ticket agent told me.

"What does that mean?" I asked.

"It means that the flight has been delayed," came his response, weary of his need to be redundant to such a dummy as me.

"What time is it scheduled to leave?" I asked.

"It will be posted. Just watch the monitors," he said, pointing to the overhead TV monitors.

"What time are they projecting it to leave?" I pressed.

"I do not have time to discuss it," came his final response.

"You don't have *time* to discuss it?" I wanted to ask him. "What do you have *time* to do?"

He turned and looked at the other ticket agent, and they resumed their discussion of who knows what, hoping, I suppose, that passengers would keep their questions to a minimum until they got off work.

IN SUMMARY

In this chapter we thought about solving the problem.
We learned that when we:

1. *Understand* the problem,
2. *Identify* the cause, and
3. *Discuss* the possible solutions,

we set the stage for problem resolution. Then all we have to do is remove the cause or take corrective action and the problem gets solved.

I suggested that it's the *attitude* and *manner* in which we remove the cause or take corrective action that helps us win with customers. An honest, conscientious desire to create value for people is demonstrated in our actions, and customers usually get the message. Our intentions and attitudes are communicated in powerful, unconscious ways.

I also mentioned the need to follow up and make sure people are satisfied with the problem resolution. It's here that our willingness to become vulnerable to their judgment or appraisal helps us impress and cement relationships with customers.

HOW TO GET GOOD AT SOLVING PROBLEMS

1. Remove the cause, or
2. Take corrective action.
3. Ask if the customer is satisfied with the resolution.

SOMETHING TO THINK ABOUT

Solve few or small problems and you'll receive small pay. Solve bigger problems and you'll earn bigger dollars. You'll usually be paid consistent with your willingness and ability to solve problems.

PHILOSOPHIES OF PROBLEM SOLVING THAT YOUR COMPETITORS WILL LOVE FOR YOU TO PRACTICE

Learn and practice the following philosophies of problem solving and complaint resolution and you'll have the friendliest competitors in town. They'll like you and do everything possible to keep you in your present job. Yeah, just adopt these guidelines and they'll love you forever.

1. Admitting a mistake is a sure sign of weakness.
2. Give in to a customer too easily and they'll take advantage of you.
3. Act too eager to assist customers and they won't respect you.
4. Be sincere and polite and customers will think you're not very competent and that they can put anything over on you.

DAILY SUCCESS DIARY
SOLVE THE PROBLEM

When you take "ownership" of problems you take the responsibility of solving them. Not only a skill, this is also an attitude. It's silently saying to customers, "I'm here to solve your problems and deliver satisfaction to you!"

This week, as you focus on these action guides, rate your performance. Doing this will help you get better and better at making customers happy.

	S	M	T	W	TH	F	S
Solve the Problem							
1. Remove the cause, or							
2. Take corrective action.							
3. Ask if the customer is satisfied with the resolution.							
Total each day							
Daily average per week							

Chapter 12

INSURING YOUR FUTURE SUCCESS

"YOUR OPPORTUNITIES ARE UNLIMITED WHEN YOU SATISFY ME!"

Your customers pay your salary! Yeah, when the dust settles you'll always get paid consistent with the value you give customers.

Whatever you do, wherever you are, it's a pretty safe assumption that you'd like to enjoy your job more, earn more money, or get a better job.

Hey, who wouldn't like to enjoy greater success?

The truth is that you have unlimited opportunities, beginning right where you are, when you realize that your success will rise to the degree that you satisfy customers.

That's the law!

The quality and quantity of value you give people will come back to you in the form of increased pay, promotion, or appreciation.

This being true, you can take control of your future success by:

1. Deciding now on the level of success you want to enjoy, then

2. Determining the value you're willing to give that will cause people to ultimately pay you more.

Now before I go on, let me ask you: What's your response to what I just told you? Do you believe me? Or do you doubt?

Hey, I'm a grown man. I've been around the block a few times. I know, for instance, that many people go to and from their jobs each day feeling stuck. Stuck in situations where they see no future, are unhappy, and don't feel appreciated.

Yeah, I know that. I've gone into many offices, banks, stores, or other businesses and seen people whose eyes have lost the excitement of what they're doing. I've conducted seminars for companies whose people just sat there saying with their blank stares, "My body may be here, but my mind is at the beach."

I realize there are many people who don't exactly get up each morning fired up with the zeal of a new day's opportunities.

YOU'RE SURROUNDED BY "INSURMOUNTABLE OPPORTUNITIES"

The sad truth is that many people don't know that their opportunities are unlimited when they focus on satisfying customers. They don't realize how their income levels will rise as they give greater levels of satisfaction to people.

Pasquale "Pat" Pagliuca discovered this truth over the years.

Born into an old-world Italian family in New York City, Pat worked for IBM as an executive secretary and then found his way to Phoenix in 1971 because of arthritis.

When he moved to Phoenix he got a job with an office supply company. His long love affair with fountain pens that began during his years as an executive secretary showed itself in the office-supply store. He found himself selling fine, expensive Mont Blanc and Waterman pens, and in the ensuing years developed quite a following of business and professional people.

In 1987 the store owner allowed Pat to set up his own company, Pens International, in the office-supply store, but a couple of years later disaster struck, and the store was forced to close its doors forever.

"I found myself totally devastated, both mentally and financially," the 48-year-old father of eight explained.

But it was then that his good customer service and trust relationships with people came to his aid. One of his customers, a wealthy man, heard of his problem and suggested a solution. The solution was to set Pat up in business in the lobby of a very up-scale office building in the center of Phoenix's financial district.

So, now, positioned between a very nice restaurant and a jewelry store, sits Pat's shop, Pens International. Looking every bit as elegant as a Fifth Avenue Cartier-type shop, expertly decorated in dark mahogany and glass, it's here that Pat holds court.

His clientele could fill a book of Who's Who, from lawyers, doctors, top executives of major corporations to sports celebrities to famous entertainers.

What's his secret of success? Listen as he tells us

"I've always had the attitude that these pens I sell can be acquired anywhere. So when customers buy from me, I owe them something besides just the pens. I owe them the best service possible. I make sure they leave happy."

Pat cites a comment one customer made about him: "Buying a pen from you, besides the purchase itself, is like starting a relationship."

Many of his old customers are now bringing their children in—as young as 10 or 11—to get their first fine fountain pen.

Recently the wife of a very well-known writer, whose name most of the people in the whole United States would recognize, came in to purchase some new pens from Pat. Returning to her home in California, she wanted to fax Pat a note of gratitude. When she discovered that he didn't have a fax machine she purchased one and sent it to her mother, who then delivered it to Pat as a gift. She did this voluntarily—as her way of thanking him for the courtesy and service he'd given her.

Wow! That's what customer satisfaction is.

Pat sums up his business philosophy by saying, "More important than the units of pens I sell are the friendships made and kept and most important, the loyalty of my customers."

In interviewing Pat, I found a genuine professional, happy with his life, thrilled and appreciative of the opportunities he had been given, and a person whose actions and relationships with people helped create his opportunities.

Oh, yes, he sent me a handwritten note of appreciation for buying a Waterman pen from him.

Pat's example models a truth that we're all surrounded by opportunities that can usher in greater levels of success and achievement.

What Opportunities Are All Around You?

As you think of this subject, let me put you on the spot and ask you a most important question. "In what ways can you create more and greater value for people that would set unseen forces into motion to bring you greater success and self-fulfillment?"

That's the golden question! The one that when asked and answered can torch the booster rockets of your climb to success.

THE LAW OF PSYCHOLOGICAL RECIPROCITY

There's a Universal, Dynamic Law that when understood and lived out in our daily actions unfailingly leads us to greater wealth and happiness. It always works over the long haul. It is only our selfish, ego-driven, "now" orientation that blinds us from enjoying the rewards of this great Law.

The essence of the Law is: Create more and better value for people and it will be returned to you in like measure. The rule is, we always get back what we give out.

Now, while it seems to me that we all know this truth from an interpersonal dimension, we fail to grasp its power when applied to our own careers and livelihood. The rough-and-tumble rat race that characterizes many people's lives deludes them into believing that life is a "take all you can get and give as little as possible" battle.

Well, it isn't! These people have believed a lie! They're sadly on the wrong track.

The truth is that our noble desires to create greater value for people, when accompanied by our daily actions, elevate us to higher levels of understanding and consciousness. Our success then trails alongside this rise. Yes, the street vendor in the crowded, grimy streets of New York who sees what he does as adding value to people's lives has by that attitude raised life to a higher, more noble plane. And he is more successful, because success has more to do with our own fulfillment with anything else.

Milton Price, who operates a shoe-shine stand in the Marriott Hotel in Des Moines, is in a league all by himself. No one in the whole galactic system gives a better shine than Mr. Price does. No one!

Mr. Price discovered many years ago that people don't come to him just to get their shoes shined; rather they come in to receive positive inspiration and encouragement.

When they come to see him they leave feeling better. He gives them emotional shoe shines. He knows everyone's name, and uses it. He knows what they do. He knows about business conditions. People confide in him.

Never lost for words, he is a treat to talk to. Calling himself a "Doctor of Shoeology," he does things with shoes that I've never seen before. After he applies his magic, you look at your shoes and say, "Wow!"

Mr. Price posts no prices. When you ask him how much you owe him, he'll reply, "Whatever it's worth to you."

And since it's obviously worth a lot, you pay him a lot—which, of course, he knows beforehand, and that's OK because his primary motive is to do a superb job. He probably earns more per pair of shoes shined than 99 percent of all the people who shine shoes in the world.

He well understands the Law of Psychological Reciprocity and plays by its rules. The Law then pays him back, as it always does.

TEAMWORK HAS MANY ADVANTAGES

Great customer service is usually the result of teamwork—people and departments working together in a spirit of co-operation and harmony. This then creates a new power.

Synergism, or the whole being greater than the sum of the individual parts, is seen in most great teams. Its magic works in many ways...and distributes its benefits to all team members by increasing their happiness, productivity, and self-esteem.

Synergism is an interesting concept. Scientists are still trying to understand and measure it.

I read a story once that illustrates the power. Most of us have seen the cleaning detergent, 20 Mule Team Borax. Remember the picture on the box?

It's a drawing of 20 mules pulling two huge wagons and a smaller one out of a borax pit in California in the 1800s. I saw this for years before I knew the significance of the picture. I was fascinated when I learned the true, little-known story.

It seems that for years the hearty wagoneers used 12 mules to pull out the wagon load of borax from an open pit. For a long time no one questioned it. But then a creative thinker, who wasn't content to live with the status quo, began experimenting. He soon found out that he could add 8 mules to the 12-mule team and with 20 mules could pull *two* huge wagons, plus a water wagon.

What that means is that by adding 8 mules to the 12 it more than doubled the pulling capacity. It created a new power

That's synergism—where two or more people or forces work together in a cooperative spirit, the combined efforts become more than the sum of the individual parts.

What's that got to do with customer service? Plenty!

Take for instance when a group of credit unions installed our Customer program with their employees, their *teller error* dropped 40 percent. Yes, 40 percent. And the accuracy of tellers wasn't even a subject in our curriculum. The teamwork created this effect.

Or how about in a group of auto dealers when we got the service, sales, and administrative people pulling together, the repair-order dollar averages went up 30 percent, and the body-shop estimate closures increased almost 50 percent. The overall profitability rose proportionally.

All these benefits happened, not just because the people learned new skills, but mainly because of the newly energized teamwork—the synergism that was created by teamwork.

The good news of all this is that as groups become more effective, each individual enjoys increased benefits, such as increased self-esteem, pride, and confidence—not to mention frequent raises and increases in pay.

Internal customers

This is why we hear so much today about external and internal customers. External customers are obvious. Everyone knows who they are.

But internal customers aren't so obvious because we haven't traditionally used this language. But accounting's internal customers may be production or marketing or shipping. Everyone serves other people within the same organization. Everything is a partnership. Everything needs to be teamwork.

Teamwork provides us with satisfaction that we don't get otherwise. Being a part of a team provides rewards of increased abilities, enjoyment, and support.

How can you give extra value so you can get paid more?

As we near the end of this book, and after you have learned the Customer-Satisfaction System and the Problem-Solving

Formula, the big question is, "What will you now do with what you've learned?"

Or, "What will you do now to assimilate and apply the processes you've learned?"

How to Assimilate and Apply These Processes

Merely reading this book will do you little good! That's a fact. As (gulp) brilliantly written as it is, if all you do is read it you'll enjoy few benefits.

Knowing information, or having knowledge, is passive and of little value until it finds its way through your actions and is lived out in habits and automatic responses.

There is a way that you can take the information in this book and program it into your mind so it's translated into action. I've mentioned it before. Let's think about it again.

Now that you've read through these pages and have a grasp of what's in them, follow these suggestions and you'll experience some wonderful benefits of confidence and greater success.

1. Go back and reread Chapter 1. Make notes in the margins, mark up the pages with scribbling and ideas. Read that same chapter once a day for five days.
2. Write the action guides on an index card, carry it each day for a week, and practice them at every opportunity.
3. Say to yourself several times each day, "My opportunities are unlimited when I satisfy customers!"

Focusing your efforts daily with repetition and time lapse will begin to build strong habits within you.

Soon you'll practice the action guides automatically, just as you do when you breathe or comb your hair.

When these automatic responses begin to play out in your relationships with customers you'll experience some thrilling moments. First, you'll stand out in the minds of your customers, patients, clients, or whatever you call them. They'll notice you above and beyond other people who do what you do.

You'll immediately feel their respect and appreciation, which will cause giant boosts of confidence to grow within you. They'll want to come back to see you, or call you, as well as send their friends to you.

Your overall prosperity will swell because you've taken responsibility for your own success and have taken the initiative to profit from the Great Law of Prosperity.

Soon, you'll earn more money, get a promotion, or enjoy greater confidence from your management.

All these seeds that you plant will sprout and grow—causing greater success, confidence, and prosperity to come into your life.

IN SUMMARY

I challenge you to take an honest look at who and where you are. To discover the opportunities that lie closely in front of you. Whether it's in your current job or another one, businesses are waiting to reward people who give customers more and greater value than they receive elsewhere.

The processes and systems in this book will help you give more and better value. They work best, and even in multiplied ways, when they're coupled with positive attitudes and values. When you *want* to serve customers better, and you do it mainly because you *feel good* about it, you'll add a rich dimension of self-assurance to your life.

As you plant the seeds of prosperity—consciously giving a greater quality and quantity of value to people, you'll enjoy thrilling new levels of success and prosperity.

By starting where you are now and practicing the ideas in this book, you'll gradually steer your passage to an exciting new future.

Test me! Try it and see!

And as you do, be kind to yourself. Enjoy every day as a gift of God. Make the most of it by helping the people you meet feel extra special.

You'll enjoy rich rewards.

You'll insure your future success!

HOW TO GET GOOD AT SATISFYING CUSTOMERS

1. Go back and reread Chapter 1. Read it once a day for five days.
2. Write the action guides on an index card, carry it each day for a week, and practice them at every opportunity.
3. Go through each chapter the same way—spending a week on each one—practicing the action guides.

SOMETHING TO THINK ABOUT AND DO

Say to yourself several times each day, "My opportunities are unlimited when I satisfy customers!"

Index

People skills
  and customer satisfaction,
    98-99
  nature of, 98-99
Persuasion, listening as
  form of, 63-64
Poor customer service
  examples of, 5-6, 12-13,
    13-14, 23-24, 27-28, 154
  methods for alienation of
    customers, 132
  and preoccupation, 13-14
Preoccupation
  breaking while listening,
    58-60
  meaning of, 14
  and poor customer
    service, 13-14
Problems
  and alienation of
    customers, 132
  nature of, 122-124
Problem solving
  compensation and size of
    problem, 120
  costs of unresolved
    complaints, 141-144
  daily success diary, 133,
    150, 180
  formula for, 121

guidelines for, 149
identification of cause of,
  137-140, 144, 146
and listening, 156-157
negative emotions related
  to, 126-127, 140
and nondefensive
  listening, 145-146
philosophies of problem
  solving, 179
and sales person, 78
taking ownership of
  problem, 127-129, 131,
  140
understanding the
  problem, 124-126
See also Solutions to
  problems

Q

Questions
  closed-ended questions,
    45-46
  to identify customer
    needs, 42, 45-46, 50
  open-ended questions,
    45-46
  and problem-solving, 127